LET'S TALK ABOUT ADOPTION

LET'S TALK ABOUT ADOPTION

Susan and Elton Klibanoff

Little, Brown and Company Boston Toronto

For John, Jennifer and Daniel,
with love

FIRST EDITION

T10/73

Library of Congress Cataloging in Publication Data

Klibanoff, Susan, 1945-
Let's talk about adoption.

Includes bibliographical references.
1. Adoption--United States. I. Klibanoff, Elton, 1943- joint author. II. Title.
HV875.K58 362.7'34'0973 73-10401
ISBN 0-316-49845-9

Published simultaneously in Canada
by Little, Brown & Company (Canada) Limited

PRINTED IN THE UNITED STATES OF AMERICA

Contents

Introduction 3

OUR STORY—A MOTHER'S-EYE VIEW

1. Before Our Baby Came 9
2. The First Year 17

WHO WANTS TO KNOW ABOUT ADOPTION

3. The Prospective Parents 29
4. The Adopted Child 41
5. Siblings and Friends 54
6. Relatives and the Community 64

HOW ADOPTION HAPPENS

7. The Biological Mother and Father 75
8. Adoption through an Agency 84
9. Independent Adoption 95
10. Children in Foster Care 104

ALL KINDS OF ADOPTION

11. Transracial Adoption 115
12. The Child with Special Needs 127
13. Older Children 140
14. Single-Parent Adoption 154
15. International Adoption 163

SOME HISTORY AND LEGAL CONTROVERSY

16. The History and Nature of Adoption 177
17. When the Biological Mother Changes Her Mind 186
18. When an Unwed Father Wants the Child 192
19. When Biological Parents Abuse, Neglect or Abandon the Child 198
20. When There Are Religious Restrictions 205

EPILOGUE

21. The Future of Adoption 217

APPENDIX A
Adoptive Parent Groups 227

APPENDIX B
Model By-Laws of an Adoptive Parents' Organization 242

APPENDIX C
Model Reform Laws
1. Uniform Surrender Document and Procedure Making the Surrender Irrevocable Once Executed 249
2. Procedure for Terminating the Right of Parents to Consent to Adoption 251
3. Rights of the Unwed Father 253
4. Financial Subsidies to Adoptive Parents 254
5. Tips for Legislative Reform 255

Notes to Chapters 259

Acknowledgments

WE wish to give special thanks to Donald and Betsy Anderson, Phyllis Cosand, Dr. Eric Denhoff, Ann Gillis, Associate Justice Edmund Keville, Marty and Grace Lerman, Fred and Carol Miller, Jim and Judy Meredith, Phyllis Oram, Frank Sander, Ann Smith, Lurana Snow and Carol Trust for advice and information they have given us about adoption and related subjects. Many, many others have helped us as well, even though they may not always have known it at the time. For their experiences, thoughts and feelings, we say thank you, too. We also want to thank Charles Burnett for his time and lovely photograph.

Sue Swain had the unenviable but essential job of typing the manuscript, parts of it more than once, and tolerating Elton's handwriting. Love and thanks for that.

Finally, we want our parents and Nancy Granfors to know that we appreciate the afternoons and weekends of baby-sitting which gave us time to write.

And a woman who held a babe against her bosom said, Speak to us of Children.

And he said:

Your children are not your children.

They are the sons and daughters of Life's longing for itself.

They come through you but not from you,

And though they are with you yet they belong not to you . . .

—Kahlil Gibran
from "On Children" in *The Prophet*

LET'S TALK ABOUT ADOPTION

Introduction

ALTHOUGH the introduction is what you read first in a book, we are writing ours last. We have written the chapters, setting out our feelings, ideas and suggestions. And now we find ourselves at the beginning once again.

We began this project because we felt that, as a whole, the general public is ignorant about adoption – we still feel that way. And yet if you consider that 175,000 children were adopted just in the year 1970 in the United States, there's a large group of people who in one way or another are directly connected with it.

In addition, adoption indirectly touches the lives of all people, regardless of whether or not they are adoptive families, and as we finish our writing, we hope that everyone will want to learn about adoption.

We not only want our readers to know about it for their own information or enlightenment. We want them to know because of the children. The ones who wait for homes, as well as the ones who have already been brought together with their families. If adults are insensitive to children's feelings – for whatever reasons – or are unaware of the homeless children in the world today, it is the children who suffer. It may be a trifle idealistic, but wouldn't it be nice if all adults came to think of adoption as good and natural – which it is! We cannot change the past for many people, adults and children alike, but why dwell on it? Let's work for a better today and tomorrow.

What can be learned from reading this book? We'll answer that with a series of questions.

Do you know why people adopt? Where to go if you want to adopt? Do you know the difference between independent and "black market" adoption? Can you discuss adoption with a child who was adopted – or with one who wasn't? Can you discuss adoption with your neighbors?

Did you know that single persons adopt children? Do you have questions about transracial adoption, or adopting children with special needs? What about adopting older children or children from other countries?

Do you know the difference between adoption and foster care? Do you know anything about the rights of the biological parents; do you know anything about what they think or feel? Are you worried about whether your child's first mother might come back someday? Or what if your child sets out to find her?

See. There's much more to adoption than whispering about it and pointing at some child, saying, "He's adopted." Much, much more.

There are a few things we want our readers to be aware of before they read the book:

1. Our suggestions are based on our own feelings, and are given as guidelines, not gospel. Each person or family has its own lifestyle; we hope our readers will think for themselves, based on their own needs, about things they've never thought about.

2. Adoption has become a negative word. It has come to mean a difference, something that sets a family apart from others, rather than an alternative way of having a family. We use the word often because this is what our book is about. We hope the book will help change the connotation.

3. We don't believe adoption is special, adopted children vulnerable, or adoptive parents noble. We're very proud of our children, but we love and nurture them because of what and who they are, not because of how each may have come into our family. Many people believe in the "specialness" of adoption, or various kinds of adoption. But we feel that each family is of special value and unique in itself.

4. Not everyone will believe or like all we say. Fine with us. We just ask for openmindedness.

Who are we? and what gives us the authority to write this book? In the first two chapters you can read about our family and how our interest grew. Essentially, we are parents, and we're writing from that viewpoint. What we have to say comes from our experiences as parents raising children, and from those people who have crossed paths with us through the years. We have listened and learned from adoptive and non-adoptive families, social workers, professional colleagues, unwed mothers and fathers, friends and neighbors. We've been involved with public policy, adoption legislation, and adoptive parents' organizations. We've spent much time talking with and learning from one another. We're writing now because we feel we have something to share with others, and because we feel there is a need for what we have to say. We hope you enjoy the book and make some of it part of you.

OUR STORY –
A MOTHER'S-EYE VIEW

1/ Before Our Baby Came

"HELLO, Mrs. Klibanoff?"

"Yes."

"This is Miss James. We have a baby for you."

I cannot remember what I said after a long period of silence on my end of the phone. I do recall trying very, very hard to sound calm as I wrote what she told me about the baby on a piece of yellow paper napkin lying on the table.

It is easy to imagine a man being told in a hospital corridor: "Congratulations, you have just become a father." It is much more difficult to picture a woman who hasn't been pregnant being suddenly told: "Congratulations, you have just become a mother!" It is an amazing – and wonderful – feeling.

That telephone call was the culmination of many long months of waiting and learning. Adoption is a subject my husband and I had discussed through the years. We had borne one child, our son John, and felt that after our next two children – which we were positive would be boys – we would adopt a baby girl. We were not prepared, therefore, to find ourselves among the ranks of "infertile" couples a few years, and many expensive medical bills, later.

We were both in our mid-twenties, and although our chances were slim, we could have continued to try to have a child through pregnancy, but we wanted to increase our family then. Our happiness was definitely beginning to suffer as the result of two and one half years of trying to conceive. We sat down one evening and decided to investigate the possibilities of adopting a baby.

It was at this point that we realized how little we knew about adoption. We weren't positive how to go about finding an agency, and we never dreamed that there might be laws which would hinder our efforts. A social worker we knew suggested two agencies I might call, and I remembered the name of a third, let's call it "The Boston Children's Society," from my childhood. My parents would drive past the building and tell me it was the place where the orphans live. I would peer out the window, and try to catch sight of some little child in tattered clothing. Sentiment prevailed, and I placed my first call to the Children's Society. I said I wanted to adopt a baby and asked to be mailed an application form.

No, they were sorry, but there was a procedure that had to be followed. We must first make an appointment for a "preliminary group interview." It was now July and their earliest unfilled meeting was at the end of September! At that time, we would be given an application, which we would mail back. It did not matter how strongly I knew I wanted to adopt, rules were rules. After the application was received, there would be a wait of almost a year until the "home study" began. When it was completed and we were accepted, a baby would be placed in our home within a few months.

My head spun with all the new terms with which I would soon become familiar, and I was disappointed by the length of the wait. I'm afraid endurance has never been one of my better qualities. I placed a second telephone call, this time to the Jewish family agency in our area.

Once again, I would have to make an appointment for a preliminary interview for both my husband and myself before we could apply. The time from application to placement of a child was likely to be at least two years, possibly three or more. I made an appointment anyway – for October.

I called the third agency, a small one in a nearby town. This time I was totally surprised (based on my "extensive" experience) to be asked my religion. I inquired what relevance that might have, since my husband and I did not care about the religious background of a baby. At this, the lady with whom I was speaking explained in an extremely solicitous manner that in Massachusetts there were laws prohibiting the adoption of a child of one religion by parents of another. (The religion of the baby is considered to be that of the woman who bore it.) There were a few agencies that accepted religious "waivers" from the biological mother, but this agency did not. Moreover, if I were Jewish, I might as well look elsewhere since there were very few Jewish babies, and this agency did not handle them.

I could not believe all the problems I had run up against, and felt a need to discuss them with someone. My husband knew no more than I did, so we decided to talk with Debbie, a friend who was a social worker for the state, working with foster children. I now realize how lucky we were, because many people have no such acquaintance, and literally suffer in silence. She came to our home that evening, and our enlightenment began.

We first discussed the religious problem. I was offended that such a law existed in 1968. A few agencies avoided its apparent restrictiveness with the religious waivers. These are documents a mother signs at the time she releases her baby for adoption, and they state that the mother will allow the child to be placed in a home of any religion. To my relief, Debbie knew that the Children's Society used the waivers.

We were surprised that it took so long to adopt a baby, for we had thought that there were more children available for adoption than families for them. Debbie explained that there were now more families interested than babies available, and a year to a year and a half was a reasonable time to have to wait. Also, many agencies were understaffed, further adding to the delay.

Summer turned to fall, and we went to the preliminary group meeting at the Children's Society. Apprehensive at first, I came away feeling fairly confident. My husband, who usually has a more positive attitude than I do, never felt my new concern that we might be rejected because we already had one child. The meeting was led by a patronizing middle-aged social worker who explained that there would be a nine-month wait for the home study to begin. At that time, we would be assigned a case worker who would interview us both jointly and separately for a variable number of visits. If there were already children in the family (I inwardly sighed when I heard this), the worker would also like to meet the child. Five references were required, as well as letters from physicians with relevant data about fertility. (I might say here that each agency has its own requirements about reference letters.) We could mail the application anytime, and they would be acted upon in the order they were received. A total of six couples were at the meeting, and I remember wishing I had a stamp so we could mail our application immediately.

Everything was straightforward. All we had to do was wait.

A month passed and we went to the preliminary interview at the Jewish agency, but learning that the wait would be even more than the predicted two years, since we already had a child and they had very few babies, we did not apply.

I looked in the library and bookstores, and although I found several books that dealt with adoption, none of them was able to answer to our satisfaction the questions my husband and I had been discussing with one another. How should we tell our son about adoption? Is there one best way to do it? How would we tell our adopted child about adoption as he or she grew? They wouldn't really check under the beds, would they? What if we were turned down?

I do not want to cause any person, especially a social worker, who has just read the last paragraph to cringe — this is not going to be another one of those books that talk about "special" babies and how lucky the "poor little things" are to be taken in. I want the reader to see adoption through unsentimental and unprofessional eyes.

As winter turned to spring, we heard of an agency where it took only two to three months to adopt a baby. A call to the agency confirmed this, and my husband and I made an appointment for the first interview. I still had found no books that were helpful, and the woman I spoke with said she would mail us a list – she never did. Our interview came and went, and we were told we would receive a letter in one month telling us when the home study would begin. Our next communication from this agency was a telephone call fifteen months later.

It had been a busy spring, and adoption concerns did not consume all our energies. My husband started a new job in the governor's office; I had a part-time job which I enjoyed; our son was finishing nursery school and getting ready for his first summer of day camp. I decided I had reached a point at which I could no longer agonize, or else my mental health would suffer. We kept busy, and soon it was August.

In the middle of August, approximately one month earlier than we expected, a social worker, Miss James, called from the Children's Society, and our long-awaited home study began. Our first interview was a joint one, during which we discussed our medical history, our marriage, our son John, and our feelings about adoption. She was young and pleasant, and we found it easy to talk with her. Miss James also asked if we had any special requests about a baby. My husband and I had heard that some agencies do ask this, and we had discussed this ourselves. Our only request would be for a girl. Although we wanted a large family, if for some reason we decided to limit our growth to two children, it would be nicest to have one boy and one girl, and we stated this. Educational background, ancestry, and religion of the baby's biological parents did not matter to us.

A week later, we each had a separate interview. She went over what we had previously discussed, and asked if we had any further questions at that time. We didn't, and the last remaining part of the home study was to be Miss James's meeting with John. For this, she came to our home.

I remembered that at our first group meeting, the social worker who conducted it said that many times parents clean so thoroughly for the social worker's visit that there aren't even any toys in sight. She considered this unnecessary, as well as unrealistic, and urged no one to overclean for the benefit of a social worker. In all honesty, I did not overclean, although perhaps I might have if I had not felt so relaxed with Miss James.

John knew vaguely that someone who had something to do with adopted babies (I will discuss in another place telling John about adoption) would be coming to our house, and we felt this was sufficient preparation for him. Miss James arrived at three, and it was a struggle to get John to leave his friends outdoors and come in long enough to be even slightly sociable. The promise of a soda and some cookies finally persuaded him, and we all sat down at the kitchen table. After talking with John about his interests, his toys, and school, Miss James innocently asked him if he knew anything at all about adopted babies. "Oh, yes," John just as innocently answered. "They come from teenage girls who aren't married and can't keep them."

She looked at me, I looked at her, and we both turned to John. I was amazed, and asked my son, who was then all of four and three quarters years old, where he had learned that. His answer: from the baby-sitter!

The rest of the afternoon was anticlimactic, and Miss James left saying there would be no problem with our acceptance, and we would receive a telephone call in two to three days saying we were officially accepted. I would have preferred something more tangible, like a letter, but our long wait appeared to be nearing an end, and I decided I did not need the extra security a letter would represent.

We received the promised call, and Miss James told us that the wait for a baby girl would be from three weeks to three months. The panel of social workers that decides which babies are appropriate for which families met every second Friday morning, and she would call us on a Friday afternoon.

We busied ourselves erecting the crib and doing some basic layette shopping. There is a distinct advantage in knowing the sex of a baby before it arrives. Our son had spent the first several months of his life surrounded by yellow: yellow kimonos, yellow blankets, even a yellow diaper pail! Our little girl would not have to suffer the fate of the ambiguous baby – everything would be pink!

Three weeks later, on a Friday afternoon, I made a conscious decision to stay home and do some reading. Logically, I felt it was too soon to expect the call, but I wanted to be home just in case. I became deeply involved in my book, and was not thinking about babies when the telephone rang and I went to answer it.

"Hello, Mrs. Klibanoff?"

2/ The First Year

THE time from Friday afternoon to Monday morning stretched on and on interminably, but at last Monday came, sunny and bright. As the three of us drove quietly to the Children's Society to get our new baby, we were each nervous in our own way. Elton wondered what she would look like; I wondered how she would feel when I hugged her; and John worried about his new status in the family.

We were ushered into a sitting room, and sat side by side on the sofa as Miss James went to get the baby. Certain that I would cry, I was amazed to find myself calm and relaxed as I was handed a pink blanket with a tiny little head and big brown eyes peering from it. She was beautiful! Just a soft little thing lying there, and she was ours. We took turns holding her, and watching her watch us, till after about half an hour, the four of us went home.

We decided to stop at a card shop for birth announcements to mail to friends and relatives. As we sifted through the racks to find just the right one, a helpful saleslady came to ask if she could help. In the manner of most females, she looked down into the blanket I was carrying, and "oohed" and "aahed" over the baby. She turned to John and said, "Don't you love your new sister?" (A risky thing to say to any child!) John looked up and said, "Yes. She's adopted." The woman looked back for a second peek at Jennifer. "Tch, tch, poor little thing. What wonderful people you must be to take her in."

The lady grabbed a box and, after pushing aside the cards at the top, produced some "I Am Adopted" announcements. Everyone who has adopted a child has an opinion about this type of announcement. We had discussed it beforehand and decided that these were not what we wanted. We have never felt that Jennifer should have a label attached to her. There is no need for "adoption" announcements or "adopted" baby books. She is not our "adopted" daughter; she is our daughter who came into our family by means of adoption. There is a big difference. We chose simple announcements that pictured a little baby girl in a cradle, with eyes as big as Jennifer's. It said simply "I'm here." Inside, where it said "date of birth" we printed the date of birth, and beneath hand-printed "date of arrival," the date we picked her up. The saleslady smiled and we left the store.

We told our family and friends that we wanted to spend our first day as a family alone and asked that they visit the next evening instead – John's birthday. The day passed quietly, with a trip to the pediatrician to check and make sure that Jennifer was healthy.

One other incident happened that first day, when we telephoned the diaper service company. The lady taking down the information asked me where the baby had been born. I was silent at first, and finally said, "I don't know.

We adopted her." For the second time in less than four hours I was told how wonderful I was, how marvelous it is that people would do something like "that."

As we discussed the day's events, both Elton and I wondered how many other people had feelings like those of the card-shop and diaper-service ladies but did not express them to us. We decided to keep a journal of events and maybe someday do something with it to help change the attitudes we encountered. We had no idea at the time how deep our involvement with adoption would become in the ensuing months.

John was very anxious to show off his new sister. The next morning, he took one of his little birthday crowns to put on Jennifer's head. He announced she was the official "princess." The grandparents, aunts and uncles arrived later in the day, bearing gifts for everyone. We all were very happy. John showed the relatives where Jennifer slept and they were all very curious about what she looked like. Although John was very proud of his responsibility, he was really pleased when everybody sang "Happy Birthday" just to him.

Time passed and each of us dealt with the adoption in his own way. For us, "dealing" with the adoption essentially meant getting used to the new person in our home. Like any experience that is new and different in one's life – especially a new person – adjustment takes time. After several days of being sure we would drop or break her in some way, we felt more relaxed. I was once again the confident, experienced mother, handling her like a favorite football, tucked nonchalantly under my right arm. Elton was once again affectionately known as "dumper Daddy" since he was in charge of disposing of the messy diapers in a manner I never could equal. He was more surprised and disoriented by the fact that she was the first female baby he had any responsibility for than he was by her adoption. And John had the totally new experience of being a brother.

After at least four weeks of hearing John say how "wonderful" the new baby was and how much he loved her, we felt it was time for a reassuring talk. We sat down and told him that there was no need for him to tell us all the time how much he loved Jennifer. She was new in the house and it would take time to grow to love her. Just because she was his sister did not mean he had to love her instantly. He looked at us and said, "You mean it?" We told him we did and he was able to relax and settle down into a normal sibling rivalry.

Occasionally, John would test us to make sure Jennifer was a permanent member of the family. During one Sunday drive, Jennifer was being particularly fussy. John sat watching her fuss and cry for a while, then announced he knew what her problem was. "She's crying because she misses her mother." Elton and I were both silent, somewhat startled by his statement. Then I recalled the advice of a friend who had told me that her daughter had said a similar thing when she had adopted a baby. Quite carefully I told John: "I am her mother now, and that is not why she's crying. Her diapers must be quite wet and it's her dinner time. Since she can't talk, she's using her crying to tell us to change and feed her." He was satisfied with the answer, and I was proud of myself for thinking before I replied.

Elton and I had to deal, too, with one issue which is solely an adoption problem. Truthfully, it was more my concern than his. We both knew that somewhere there was a woman who could say, "I want this baby back." From time to time we would hear of cases or read about them in the newspapers. There was a case pending in Massachusetts at the time which might have endangered all adoptive placements. We knew about it because Elton was actively involved with changing adoption laws. We realized that during the waiting period between placement and final adoption, the biological mother can cause serious legal conflict by changing her mind. Very few women do, but the possibility was upsetting to me. I said very little at first, but one night I saw a television show where a mother crept into a house in the middle of the night to see her baby one last time. Although the show was rather absurd, I decided to tell Elton how I felt. He was able to ease my mind considerably by pointing out the great efforts agencies undertake to assure that the mother's decision to surrender the child is a sound one, understood by her to be permanent. Moreover, the courts in our state had not looked favorably in the past on attempts to get children back.

As the months passed, we became aware of the great numbers of people who are adopted. When I pushed the carriage around the neighborhood or visited a friend, people would announce that their cousin was adopted, or the girl upstairs, or even their sister or brother. Two friends told us that they themselves had been adopted. Several of Elton's business associates told of having adopted children, and would whip out pictures of their kids. We listened to countless stories of why and when and how. In turn, people would ask to hear ours.

We came to realize that adoption was quite common, yet discussion of it was reserved almost totally for those who were uninhibited enough to declare that they had experienced it. There was a surprising amount of lack of knowledge and of misinformation. Although most adoptive parents felt very secure and natural about adoption, many had questions, with no idea who had the answers. One woman with four children, two adopted and two biological, introduced me to them by saying: "The oldest two are adopted and the younger ones are my own." She told me that she didn't like to distinguish them like that, but didn't know how else to say it. I suggested that, if the occasion called for an explanation, she should say that the oldest two are adopted and the younger two biological. "All of them are your own," I added. She thanked me for helping and said that the problem had been bothering her for years.

We found some parents who said that their kids were "just like our own would be." Others would make a point of mentioning to their children at practically every conceivable opportunity that they were adopted. Both approaches are intended not so much for the children, but rather for the parents to convince themselves that adoption is just as good – just as natural – as bearing children. We asked ourselves why people felt the need to say those things. Why couldn't they just believe? Adoption is natural and it is common; your family is what you make of it.

We were also quite surprised at the numbers of people who suddenly sought us out for advice. These were people who had heard about our adoption and were interested in it for themselves; they were anxious to talk with someone who had done it. Some were friends, a few were neighbors, and some were people we had never met. Usually, their questions were the same ones that we ourselves had had not so many months ago: Where do you go? What do you say? How do you pass investigation? How long must you wait? What about religion? What about our income? And many, many more.

From all these people and from others whom we sought out because of their experience and wisdom grew an adoptive-parents' group, intended to meet the great need for information, for support, and for public education. There was at the time one organization of considerable size already functioning in our state, but it had an almost exclusive interest in transracial adoption. Many of us felt that there was need for parents with broader interests to serve the needs of many people not primarily interested in that type of adoption. Over the course of four months during the latter part of this first year, a core group of several couples worked and planned an organization which would have adoption itself as the central issue. There would be branches concerned with legislation, foster care, prospective adoptive families, postadoptive families, and education of the public. Everyone involved worked toward an early first meeting.

Through some of these contacts, Elton was asked to work on a bill to change Massachusetts' outdated law regarding religion in adoptive placements. Our personal experience had made us aware of the problems created, both for prospective adoptive couples and for children awaiting placement, by the existence of these legal restrictions. We quickly learned that to encourage new ways of thinking about adoption would mean to politicize those interested in adoption reform and to educate the rest. Most people are willing to work for reform once they know a problem exists.

To return to the family – our first year after placement was a time of interest and concern about the role of the adoption agency. Policies concerning home visits differ from agency to agency and worker to worker. We had only two such visits after Jennifer came: the first when Jennifer was two months old and the second at Christmastime, when Miss James brought presents for both John and Jenny. Neither visit was noteworthy – as I recall, Jenny slept through the second. I did think that it was very thoughtful of Miss James to bring a gift for John. He, of course, always made a special connection between her and Jenny and was obviously very pleased with the evidence of his importance to Miss James as well. Her thoughtfulness meant a great deal to him.

None of us ever felt as though we were being "investigated" or "inspected" – just that a friend was coming to visit. Most home visits we have heard about are relaxed and comfortable if the parents, as well as the worker, intend them to be so. The parents must be open and trusting and ready to ask any questions they may have. It is normal to have questions, even doubts. During that first year I made several telephone calls to the agency. Once we needed to know who had authority to grant permission for minor surgery. (We found out that the agency does, in those states which do not grant legal custody or guardianship to the prospective adoptive parents.) Another time we asked if there were any legal restrictions about taking Jennifer on an extended vacation (there were none).

Finally, we asked who was responsible at that point for Jenny's medical bills (she was covered under the agency's group policy until legal adoption).

When the year had passed, and spring was again in the air, it was time to go to court. I called Miss James to ask when the great day would be. She was very casual about it, explaining that there were several couples whose adoptions were pending at the same time, and that she wanted to arrange a date convenient to all of us if that could be done. I assured her that the most convenient date for us would be the earliest one possible. In a few days, she returned our call to tell us of the arrangements and to ask that we appear at the courthouse at nine o'clock sharp on the day in question. We were instructed to bring Jennifer with us. We were to be prompt because the judge preferred to dispose of adoption cases first. Babies in the courtroom are a big distraction. All other details would be handled by the agency as part of its services. We would be expected to sign a paper, appear before the judge and then leave. It seemed very simple, almost anticlimactic. We had expected something rather more ceremonious and dramatic.

The day finally arrived. John left for first grade as usual. We decided not to mention any of this to him, since we felt he was rather young to understand about courts and law and we didn't want him to think that Jennifer hadn't belonged to us from the minute we saw her. If he had been older, we probably would have told him more and taken him with us to court.

Jenny was dressed in her prettiest smocked dress, the little wisp of hair on her head brushed, and several diapers pinned on at once to prevent leakage. We also brought cookies and two bottles of milk, in the event of a long wait.

Traffic was heavy, there were no parking spaces, but we somehow managed to arrive on time. The other couples were there and Miss James was running around with piles of papers, trying to get everyone and everything into one quiet, cohesive group.

We went into the courtroom. It was old, dingy, and filled with tired-looking people. Our little group of meticulously dressed adults and scrubbed, shiny babies seemed very conspicuous and out of place. We sat down in a little corner. When the judge called the court to order, Jennifer started to cry and fuss. All eyes turned in our direction, and I finally pushed a bottle in her mouth. The judge called Miss James to the bench and they whispered for a few minutes, glancing toward our group every so often. Finally, the judge called one couple, and then it was our turn.

We walked to the front, carrying Jennifer, who was sucking away on her bottle. We listened to the judge tell us what a nice family we looked like and offer us his congratulations. We left the courtroom a "legal" family.

WHO WANTS TO KNOW ABOUT ADOPTION

3/ The Prospective Parents

WHEN people think about adoption, they almost automatically associate it with an infertile couple. And, traditionally, the majority of families who have adopted children have done so because they could not biologically reproduce. After a period of trying to conceive, be it one year or ten, a couple would make the decision to adopt.

Many families still enter into adoption out of a feeling of desperation. Long months and years of doctor visits and medical bills, programs of patterned intercourse and month after month of depression have made them feel inadequate as people. Women, especially, have grown up with visions of babies and pregnancy. Long-term friendships can be temporarily disrupted or completely broken when a friend or neighbor becomes pregnant. Infertile couples with no children may even cut themselves off from families who do have children. Grocery stores and shops seem to have wall-to-wall big-bellied women, and those who aren't pregnant are toting one or two small babies in their arms. The word "baby" is part of every sentence, and half the pregnant neighbors are moaning and complaining about their unplanned "accidents." The patronizing person with an air of infinite understanding and the pushy one who asks, "Why don't you have any children?" are equally offensive.

It isn't very hard to see why infertility can be so depressing and can pervade the thoughts of a childless pair. But it can also ruin their lives, both as individuals and as a unit. This depression, and often a resulting hostility, can destroy a marriage and turn some persons into bitter human beings.

We don't pretend to be able to help such people reverse the course of their development; only self-evaluation and professional help can do that. If you are a couple stuck somewhere in this infertility quagmire, now might be a good time to take stock of your situation and consider adoption.

For some infertile couples, adoption is an easy alternative. But for many families it is definitely a second choice. For families with this attitude who have already adopted children, we hope that you will come to realize that adoption in itself is "first-best." Those of you who have yet to adopt a child but are infertile should sit down and honestly discuss your feelings about adoption. Many people don't. They think that since they have no choice but to adopt, how they feel about their adopted child won't matter. It is the only way for them to have children.

But they are wrong. A couple who considers their child second-best, or adoption second-best, will not start off as good parents. Their values are distorted. Instead of focusing on the meaning of a family, they are hung-up with the physical act of reproduction. If when they look at a child they adopt they see only the denial of biological children, it will be difficult for them to develop a healthy parent-child relationship. What should be important is not *how* the child arrived, but the fact that the child is there, and a family has been formed.

There are probably several childless couples reading this and thinking: "That's easy for you to say. You've had kids," and to some extent they are right. But there are many things – not just having children – that people are denied in life. There is no constructive purpose in being bitter about these losses, if they are not reversible. You have to be willing to say to yourself, "Here's where I am; now what can I do from here?"

Once a person reaches that point, he can start talking about his concerns and feelings about adoption. This is especially important for a couple where one spouse is either lukewarm or actively negative toward adopting a child. By recognizing and solving possible problems before the adoption, they can spare themselves and their children much heartache.

We don't want people to think that a "second-best" attitude in the beginning will mean an unsuccessful adoption later. Not so. What is important is to communicate these feelings honestly, learn as much as possible about adoption, and meet with families who have adopted children, in order to talk about their experiences. Look at the overall goals of having and raising a family. If you come to believe that children can be loved for who they are, not where they came from, the "second-best" attitude will dissolve itself in good time.

Not everyone who adopts does so because of a fertility

problem. There are many families who simply feel that they have much to share with a child who needs a home. Their efforts may be directed at the "hard-to-place" children, children with various physical, mental or emotional handicaps, mixed-racial children, black children, or children from overseas. They have learned about them through the publicity the media have given children in need, or they have friends or acquaintances who adopted in this way.

Some of the families have had contact with a particular special-needs child in either their home or work lives, and become interested in adopting because of it; there are families who wish to adopt foster children. Single persons as well as married couples express the desire to adopt. In addition, there are numbers of relative adoptions: adoptions, usually caused by the death of one or both parents, which take place within an extended family.

Deciding whether adoption is right for them provides a couple with an excellent opportunity for talking about long-range expectations for their family and for their life together. Sometimes the couple agrees that adoption is what they want, but they are unwilling or unable to discuss with one another fears, questions and thoughts on it. Here is a "beginning list" of questions for families to ask themselves and talk about before adopting.

1. Are you communicating honestly to one another your feelings about adoption? Are you holding back thoughts so you won't upset your spouse?

2. Will you be giving a child a secure home life, or do you hope he will hold the family together?

3. How will you feel toward a child you adopt if you later become pregnant?

4. Are you willing to accept him for himself—espe-

cially if he is older, or of another nationality or color? Can you be proud of him?

5. Are you adopting as your way of "saving" a child? Do you realize that this attitude by itself is not sufficient reason to adopt?

6. Do you feel depressed and desperate, or are you ready to consider adoption a positive and good experience?

As a couple enters the adoption experience, there are countless questions they want answered. Here are some of the most frequently asked ones, and some of our answers to them.

How do we find an adoption agency?

Telephone books are one source. Agencies are sometimes listed under the heading "Adoption." The state or county departments of public welfare are also a source of information. Churches and other religious organizations will know of adoption agencies (usually affiliated with their own faith). In addition, child welfare and family service agencies will have a list of resources if they themselves do not provide adoption services.

How many agencies can we contact?

A family can contact as many agencies as they choose. Talking with people at various agencies gives families the opportunity to see where they feel most comfortable, and to learn about different agency policies. Once an agency starts a home study, however, the family should withdraw its name from the other agencies, out of fairness to the other couples who are still waiting for studies.

We want a white, healthy baby, but there are none available. What can we do?

There is most definitely a baby shortage. There is not, however, a children shortage. There are thousands of children who need homes and families. Some of these children have mental, physical or emotional handicaps; some are simply no longer babies. Often there are sibling groups available. Others are children who are orphans in foreign countries, victims of poverty or war.

A couple who wants a white baby may have several years to wait. Some agencies will tell them that they will never get a baby. This is a hard blow to take, but nobody can come up with babies who aren't there. Couples must be willing to make a decision. Do they choose to remain childless, or will a child other than a baby be acceptable to them? To help decide, be open-minded enough to tell an agency that you would like to come to a meeting and hear about the children who need homes. Your decision about whether or not to wait for the white baby should be made only after you learn about the children who are available.

One avenue for the couple who insists on a white baby may be independent adoption (see Chapter 9). Often, a lawyer or doctor will be able to put you in contact with a person who can arrange an independent adoption.

Should we lie to the social worker if we think it will help?

Much of what a family does in private is its own concern, and not that of the worker. Some workers, however, are curious about matters which aren't relevant to adoption. If a question is relevant to your ability to be a good parent, always tell the truth. If a social worker seems to probe into areas unrelated to the adoption, simply tell her the subject does not seem relevant to parenthood.

This is easier to say than to do, when she has the power over whether or not you become a parent. The temptation to "stretch" the truth at certain times might be overwhelming, but remember who pays the consequences if the worker finds out!

Should we tell our children about the adoption before we do it?

By all means! Since children have a hard time with long waits, you may want to put off telling them until you have concrete details to share, depending on their age and ability to understand. Chapter 5 may be of help to you.

What will we know about a child we adopt?

If you adopt through an agency, they will give you as much relevant information as they have. They will tell about the age of the biological parents, their health, racial and national backgrounds, perhaps their religion or educational levels. Other facts that may be important to your adoption will be made known. The agency will not divulge names or addresses. The older the child, the more information there is available.

In an independent adoption, parents may sometimes learn more, depending on what the third party wants to share.

What will the biological mother know about us?

Most agencies will call the biological mother and tell her when her child has been placed in a family, if she is actively interested. Some agencies will tell her a little about the family, such as whether they live in the city or the country, and whether the family has other children. She will not be told who the family is or anything that could help her locate the child. Remember, it is a source of comfort to her to know her child will be part of a family.

The family who adopts independently stands a greater risk of having a biological mother learn where the child is. We cannot tell you what information individual third parties will share with the biological mother.

What if we don't like the baby? Can we say we don't want it, and be given another chance?

There's a certain amount of nervous worrying associated with adoption, just as there is with pregnancy. What couple isn't concerned that their child might be ugly, or turn out to be retarded, or deformed? Such fears are not limited to the childbearing couple, and a family awaiting a first child is especially vulnerable to fear of the unknown. Life has its risks, and adoption actually removes a few, in that the family knows in advance the physical and mental condition of their child. As far as looks go, no one can predict what anyone is going to look like in the future, no matter how beautiful or plain he is today. We all know plain babies who turned out to be pretty children. If a couple were to react negatively to a baby, and could verbalize their feelings, an agency would respect this reaction and not place the child with them. They may then give the family another child, or reassess whether the family should wait a bit longer, depending on the reason for the rejection.

We're not rich and don't own our house; does that matter?

Most agencies no longer look at wealth as an important factor in adoption. A family of modest means need not feel at a disadvantage. Some states even have adoption subsidy laws which make available financial assistance to families who adopt, especially those who adopt formerly "hard-to-place" children.

A friend of mine heard that you have to be between twenty-five and thirty to adopt a child. Is that true?

First, never take what your friends tell you too seriously. Often what your friends "know" is only hearsay.

We can't give you a specific answer about age restrictions. In general, couples who are within childbearing years are allowed to adopt babies. But because policies differ from agency to agency, and even from year to year in the same agency, always check for yourself with each agency you contact about their own policies.

What about cost? Isn't adoption expensive?

Once again, agency policies vary. Often their fees are based on a sliding scale, determined by the family income. Other agencies may have a flat fee for everyone, while some public agencies may have no fee at all. Most social workers will tell you that inability to pay the fee does not mean that a couple will not be able to adopt, and in some cases, as we've said, financial subsidies are available to adopting families.

In an independent adoption, the cost to the parents depends on the integrity of the third party, the one who arranges the adoption.

Mothers who adopt can't breastfeed their adopted babies, can they?

Surprisingly, yes. Producing milk does not depend on actually bearing children. There are methods of stimulating the mammary glands which enable adoptive mothers to nurse their babies. Either a physician or a local board of La Leche League can explain it to you.

We want to adopt, but we're not quite ready. Since it might take a long time, should we apply anyway?

Why not sit down and discuss why you feel you aren't ready? If you decide you can feel comfortable applying, do so. Otherwise, wait until you solve whatever is causing your indecision. It is unfair to the agency, to other prospective parents and to children who need homes to apply without real conviction.

What will happen if, after the home study, the agency says "no" to us? We know a couple who would make wonderful parents, and they were refused. Is there anything we can do if this happens?

There are couples who are refused by adoption agencies – sometimes for good cause, sometimes not. We know of many families who we feel were unjustly turned down. It is both frustrating and heartbreaking, especially when many agencies refuse to share with the couple the reason for rejection, as if they were children themselves. This reflects unfair agency policy, as does the fact that many couples are not able to reach supervisors or even the social worker after rejection. If you are turned down, try to arrange a meeting with your social worker and his/her supervisor. Discuss your feelings, and ask them if they know of anything you can do to alter their decision.

If rejected, you can still apply to other agencies. Your new choice will most likely contact the first agency to find out why you were rejected there. This doesn't mean that the second agency will also turn you down, but the road ahead will be very rocky!

Some families – a minority – are not ready to adopt. We hope that agencies will discuss their concerns about each of these families and give them guidance so that adoption might become a reality for them.

How can we find out about adoption of an older child, a child of another race, or a child with special needs?

An agency which places these children will be able to provide you with the name of a family who has already adopted such a child and would be willing to talk about it with you. Also, adoptive parents' groups include families who have adopted all kinds of children. They are your best sources of information and guidance.

What are the chances of the biological mother wanting the baby back?

If you go through a licensed child welfare agency, the chances are quite slim. The legal documents the mother has signed and the agency's rules serve to protect the adoptive family. You might want to discuss this with your particular agency, or try to find out how judges in your area have decided such cases. In an independent adoption, the adoptive parents may have less protection until the adoption is made final.

4/ The Adopted Child

WHEN a child enters his home through adoption, parents are often uneasy because of questions and situations they did not confront when they were growing up. In order to make the child comfortable with his origins and life story, adoptive parents need to learn to be relaxed and confident about them. We hope this chapter will help develop feelings of assurance.

It is relatively easy to love and hold a baby, but he becomes more challenging as he grows and explores his environment and starts questioning his parents. Most of us want our children to feel comfortable within the family unit, no matter what their age. The child's comfort at home will help him be at ease elsewhere and develop his own self-esteem.

A positive self-image is important to healthy personal growth and development. What we think of ourselves affects what we do and what we are to those around us. One's self-image begins in infancy when parents love, hold and feed their young. The more loving contact a baby receives, the more secure he feels. This security with his family is the beginning of his attitude toward himself and toward life.[1]

In some households, adoptive parents prepare themselves and their children for the first discussion on adoption by singing "adoption lullabies" from infancy and by constant use of the adjective "adopted." The theory is that the child will hear the word so often, he will be less shocked when he is told how he came into the family. If this were true, perhaps we should also sing lullabies about sex, drugs, or even toilet-training! In reality, these lullabies are most often crutches for a situation which causes the parent some stress. Whatever the reason for the stress, the lullaby will not ease discussions with a child. Often such songs will make him feel different, and not "special," as some parents would argue. All children are "special"; all children also need to "belong" to the family unit.

The opportunity to begin a discussion of adoption – one which will continue throughout childhood – will most likely occur when the child asks where babies come from. Usually, this type of question is asked between the ages of three and five, often precipitated by a visit to an expectant mother or to a new baby.

As with any important matter, the parents should be honest from the beginning. This doesn't mean overwhelming the child with more information than he can understand; it does require a simple answer addressed only to the question that is asked. For example: "All babies grow in a mommy's tummy. Some babies grow in a mommy's tummy and live and grow up with her. Other babies grow in the tummy of one mommy, and then live and grow up with another mommy and daddy who will always, always be their family. This is called adoption."

The child may or may not then ask which way he came into the family. Whether he does or not, he should be told that he is adopted. The opportunity to tell him at the same time as he learns there are two ways to have a family is too good to pass up. He is less likely to be startled than if he hears rumors outside his home; moreover, there is no reason whatever to hide his adoption from him. Most of the "horror" stories one hears about adoption stem from the fact the child was not told at an early age by his parents of his adoption. Often he finds out many years later, from a friend or relative, with damage to his self-image and hurt at the crumbling of the relationship of trust he may have developed with his parents.

After their first adoption discussion, many parents feel a sense of relief. It wasn't as difficult as anticipated, and the child usually accepts the facts as casually as he accepts any other information offered without a value judgment. After most such discussions, adoption will fall into its proper perspective for the child: one of many important subjects to be discussed with his parents.

The timing and substance of further talks about adoption will vary according to the child. A precocious youngster may have questions at an early age; so will a child who is adopted transracially and is aware of a difference in physical appearance between himself and his family. Likewise, many children calmly accept adoption, as they do sex, religion or any number of things adults may have difficulty discussing. They may go several years without mentioning adoption to their family. Often the only reference made will be the child's comment to a friend: "I was adopted when I was a baby"; or, "I grew in another mommy's tummy, and then my Mom and Dad adopted me." There is no need to pursue the issue with a child who is content with his knowledge. When he is ready, the questions will come.

We can only give guidance in answering a child's questions about adoption. Specific answers must depend on the age, intelligence and security of the child. As a parent, you know your child best and must decide how much information he is capable of absorbing. Always, however, speak in a confident and positive manner. A parent's confidence will contribute to the child's sense of well-being.

Adoptive parents report that the question "Why did you adopt me?" can be asked by a child anywhere from five to fourteen years old. A parent might well ask the child what he thinks the answer is. Such a question is rarely spontaneous. The child may have overheard a conversation in which adoption was mentioned, or a peer may have asked him about it or teased him about it. Knowing what precipitated the question often helps with the reply. Sometimes a child will say that he had been thinking about it for a long time and wanted to know – he is ready to learn more about himself.

The biology lesson is a good starting point. Remind the child that he already knows babies grow in a mommy's tummy: "Before you came, we decided we wanted a family. We knew there were two ways to have children. One way would be to grow the baby in Mommy's tummy and then raise that baby in our family." (A parent with biological children may refer to the sibling as an example of the decision to have a baby that way.) "The other choice was adoption. We would bring home and raise as our very own a child who came from another mom's tummy. We both talked a long time and decided together that we wanted to begin" (or increase) "our family by adoption."

A parent should let his child know his adoption was the result of a conscious choice, just as at another time a biological baby might have been the choice. Even if all the children in the family are adopted, the child in question should not feel he came into the family by default. Thinking he came solely because his parents couldn't bear any children is very threatening to any child, especially a young one. When he is much older he can learn about infertility if it was a contributing factor in his adoption.

A family need not go overboard and tell the child a story like: "We went to a special home and saw all the babies, and of all the babies we liked you the very best and took you home for our own." This sounds as though a puppy were being chosen rather than a son or daughter. It is over-romanticized, unrealistic and untrue. There is the additional danger that the child may fear being just as easily returned to that "special home" if his behavior displeases his parents.

A youngster will usually be quite satisfied with this story of the family and may want to hear it over and over again – just as he may want to rehear explanations of sex, religion, or why he must wear mittens in the snow.

Some parents have questioned our suggestion that the child should be told that he grew in "another mommy's tummy." They have felt uncomfortable and threatened referring to the biological mother as a mother. Some parents would prefer to say that the baby grew in another "woman's" tummy, finding this word less personal and less threatening than "mommy." They fear that the child will ask: "If she was my mommy, how can you be my mommy?" The important thing for the parents to bear in mind is that the child loves his adopted mother and will not stop loving her because he finds out that another mother gave birth to him. Children are naturally open and accepting and free from the insecurities of adoptive parents. They are better able to deal with this situation than we think and, in the long run, they will feel better about their origins by thinking of the woman who gave birth to them as a mother. The crucial factor in the child's ability to deal with the truth will be the security of his relationship with his present family. Adoptive parents need not feel threatened by referring to the first mommy as just that – they will not be rejected because of it.

But what if your child is upset when he learns that he is adopted? There is nothing you can do magically to erase his feelings. You can, however, reflect in your words and actions a positive feeling about his adoption – with your family, friends and relatives. Let him know there are many other children who were adopted and that you are happy with your family. It may take time, but his faith in the family setup will be restored by your patience and confidence.

After the first story of the family is told, more questions will begin to come. For example: "Where did I come from – how did you get me?" The parent's reply might be as follows: "When parents decide to adopt a baby, they go to a place called an adoption agency. The people there are called adoption workers. When we went, we talked with the adoption workers."

(If the child is old enough, the parent might equate talking to a doctor about family planning and conception to this experience.)

"We told them we wanted to adopt a baby" (or child) "to be part of our family and that we would soon be ready for the baby" (child) "to come. After a few months, the worker called and said our baby would be there very soon. We were so excited. We painted and fixed a room. We bought a bed and a dresser, some toys and clothes. Everyone was very happy! Then it finally was time to go and get you. We all got dressed up in our best clothes, and your brother came too. We went to the agency to pick you up. We were so happy to see you. We took you home with us just as fast as we could."

If a child is adopted independently, the story need vary only slightly: "When we decided to adopt a baby, we talked with a doctor" (lawyer, minister) "about it." From there, the story is the same.

A "mixed" family, where there are both biological and adopted children, can make the story particularly effective by drawing parallels with the process of planning and having the biological children.

The day will come when the child will ask specifically about his biological parents. Usually the question will focus on the mother, because young children are aware that babies grow in the female body and because the mother is the central parent in early childhood. The child has always felt that he belonged in the family, but at this point his security may be faltering a bit. He realizes that he came from "somewhere else," and that other people were involved. He may be uneasy when he asks about his first mother or father.

These questions are often dreaded by adoptive parents. They feel threatened by them. Unresolved feelings of inadequacy or guilt about reproductive failures often rise to the surface as the parents are reminded that other people are responsible for the existence of their child. In addition, some parents have negative feelings toward the biological mother for having conceived a child out of wedlock. These parents are often tempted to tell their child that his first parents were "sinful" or "naughty." Fortunately for the children, such parents are in the minority. While they may have good intentions – hoping to set themselves in contrast as "good" people – the child may see himself as an extension of his biological parents. Such identification is particularly likely at a time when he is showing curiosity about his origins. Parents should avoid this type of judgment; the child's self-image may be at stake.

Most adoptive parents do not know the specific reason why their child was placed for adoption. Usually they are aware that the mother was probably unmarried, and was for some reason unable to keep the baby. Therefore, the following type of conversation might be advisable.

"We will never know exactly why your mother placed you for adoption." (Try to avoid phrases like "gave you up," which have negative connotations. Once again, don't be afraid to refer to the biological mother as a mother. She was the mother once, after all.) "She was young and not married when you were born. She cared about you very much, and wanted you to have a home and a family. But she knew that she and your father could not give you that. Maybe she didn't have a job, or was still in school. Maybe she wanted to live with her mother and father. She talked with your father and she talked with people at the adoption agency" (or doctor, lawyer, or minister in the case of an independent adoption). "She said that because she cared about you, she wanted you to have a home and a family that would always be yours. The adoption agency knew we wanted a baby, and you came to our home, and we are all a family now. We will always be one.

"I know this must seem like a very sad story, and part of it is. I am sure your first mother was sad when she first talked to the adoption agency. But part of her was happy and glad, because she knew you would have your own family and always be loved. Even now, she must think about you sometimes, and you will think about her, too. She must be a very nice person."

With this simple explanation, a parent has told his son or daughter that he or she was cared for and thought about and not merely tossed aside. The child also knows that his family considers the first mother – and father – to have been good people, who considered his welfare. He may want to hear the story over and over, in an effort to put it in proper perspective in his young mind. He cannot absorb it all at once, and repetition is often his best method of learning. He may ask to find the original mother, or he may mope around and feel rather lost for a while. Love and understanding are very important to him at this time. The parents may fear rejection of themselves and their family for the unknown biological parents, but wisely will not display these emotions to their young. Biology alone does not make a family. Love, patience, and time do.

If the preceding discussion, or any other talk with a child about adoption (or, for that matter, any other important topic), proves too difficult to handle, or leads to problems with which the parent is unable to cope, he should remember that there are professional sources available to help. A pediatrician or family mental health clinic can be helpful. Family service or adoption agencies often offer counseling services after the adoption.

As a child approaches adolescence, his questions increase as his knowledge and world expand outward. He will be caught in the confusion and turmoil all teen-agers face, as his mind and body grow and mature. His thoughts about his origins are likely to change, too. For the first time, a boy may be aware of a difference in appearance from the rest of his family as he grows taller than his father, or stays short and has darker skin than his brother. A girl may suddenly be aware she is the only blonde in the family, or has freckles no one else has. If your child approaches you with these thoughts, be pleased that he is trusting enough to confide his feelings. Don't tell him that appearances don't matter, because, despite the fact that these differences may hold no importance to your family, most everything about himself holds importance to a teen-ager – any teen-ager. The simple answer that could be given a pre-adolescent is no longer sufficient. Instead, he should be told that you are aware of and approve of the differences: "We are pleased with the way you have grown."

A person's importance to himself and to others lies with his feelings, personality and behavior – not with his freckles and hairstyle. Love should not be based on physical appearance. The adoptive parent might mention that if physical appearances had been important, he would never have adopted a child. The teen-ager will be pleased that his family is talking with him in this "grown up" manner, since much of him wants to be considered an adult, and his search for acceptance will be rewarded.

At this stage of his growth, the teen-ager views sex and sexuality with renewed interest. He realizes the implications of his conception. He may feel a sense of shame, either for himself or for any of the other people involved. He may feel anger and resentment as well. If he is mature enough, the child may be understanding, especially in today's more enlightened society. His parents will have told him quite frankly that premarital conceptions and unplanned pregnancies do occur. It serves no constructive purpose to speculate on whether it was an act of love or an act of sex, or on the social impact on his biological parents. The teen-ager will not be helped by moralizing; his values are fairly well established. A sermon on the sexual habits of his biological parents, especially if made with the intent of discouraging similar behavior on the part of the child, will not be good for anyone. Parents should inspire love and trust, not fear or shame.

Although newspapers love to print articles about searches by adopted adolescents for their biological parents, most adopted children are secure enough in their family not to have any great desire to find their biological mothers and fathers.

But what if your child does come to you one day and says he wants to find his first parents? You should be sympathetic. If he is below the age of majority he most likely can't see the court records and you should tell him so. Let him know, however, that if he is still interested when he comes of age, or if your state has no such legal restriction, you'll do all you can to help. That way, you are showing your child that, no matter how difficult it is for you, your dedication to him comes before any selfish (and groundless) fear of losing him.

Any child who is old enough to try to trace his parents ought to realize that, should he somehow find them, he may not be greeted with open arms. Many unwed mothers never tell the men they later marry of their baby before marriage and it is unfair to such a mother to reintroduce a child she may not have seen for fifteen or twenty years. Some women will have families, too, and even if the husband may know of the child, the family's happiness and security may be threatened. The child can be made aware of the possible harmful consequences to others of his effort.

A trip to the adoption agency or other place where records are kept may satisfy even a strong desire for information, and the search could end there. If the desire persists, the family might consider professional counseling – for the family as well as the child. Often, the search may indicate a problem in the family relationship.

Sometimes the need to find biological parents means that the child feels rejected – a child who was adopted may believe that because there were other parents before, he has someone who will want him more, someone he can belong to once again. Before becoming judgmental and saying that "all adopted children want to find their parents," the parents should cast their eyes on themselves first. Have they, in any way, as parents, grandparents, friends or relatives, contributed to this rejection? If so, what can be done to change these attitudes, starting immediately!

We once met a woman who had adopted five children, all of whom by then were in their teens. We asked her what advice she had for adoptive parents and she said, "Kids are all different. Each of mine had his or her own questions, and I could never guess who would ask what. They are each individuals, with their own feelings and personalities, and I treat them that way. Children are human beings. It doesn't matter where they come from."

A relationship of love and trust is what produces security for an adopted child – or any child. The goal in answering questions about adoption should always be to help build that kind of relationship.

5/ Siblings and Friends

For many families there are not only adopted children who have to be told about adoption, but biological ones as well. Some were born prior to the coming of the adopted child, some after; they all need to know how adoption occurs and how natural it is.

Parents are particularly concerned with how to discuss an impending adoption with the prospective brothers and sisters. The best advice for them is to be open, honest and positive. The children will develop accepting attitudes of their own.

Chances are that the younger biological children have never heard the word *adoption* before their own family thought about adopting. This lack of knowledge will work in the parents' favor, since there will be no negative feelings to combat initially. And a child who is old enough to learn about adoption probably has some ideas about where babies come from. As we have seen, the time for beginning sex education is an ideal time for talking about adoption.

Let's assume that you are sure that you will receive a child through adoption – there is no need to explain something that might not happen.

A good time to begin is at a family dinner, when everyone is together and relaxed. You can start by saying that there are two ways a child can come into a family. You might ask: "Do you know what they are, Johnny?" Or, you can just continue and say that some children are grown in their mother's tummy, while other children are adopted into the family. Unless children think that all babies come from cabbage patches or storks, reference to "growing" a family may go unnoticed; the question will be: "Mommy, what's adopted?"

One simple answer is that a child who is adopted grew in one mommy's tummy, but will grow up and live with a different mommy and daddy. "You grew in my tummy and will always stay and live with me and Daddy." This is a good time to reinforce the permanent nature of your own family so your young children won't feel that they, too, might be given up for adoption.

You can tell your children about families who have had children both ways. Telling a youngster that a playmate or relative was adopted changes an abstract idea into a real one and makes it easier to understand.

By this time, most children will have had more than enough new information to absorb. If there are more questions, you might consider going over the material you have already discussed, and not introducing anything new. A child needs time to think and the adults need time to discuss his reactions. Even if you are somewhat anxious during this conversation, try to treat it as one more interesting topic of family conversation – not a threat to the family's status quo.

It's wise to let several days pass before mentioning adoption again, and once more, let it be part of a family discussion. After going over the first talk you had, decide whether you and your children are ready to talk more personally. You might say: "We have decided that we want to have another child. And we want this child to be adopted into our family."

Questions will come pouring in – about adoption and about the new brother or sister. The answers should be straightforward and simple. If the age and sex of the new arrival are known, the children should be told. If they ask how big the new brother or sister will be, compare him or her with a familiar child or baby for size. If the child will be of another color, tell them this too. Children should not be allowed to assume that the sibling will look like them when it won't; having a misapprehension will only make acceptance harder. Once again, honesty and openness from the start will pay off.

The children will want to share in the preparations for the new arrival. They can help pick out stuffed animals and a layette for a new baby, or help get a bed and toys ready for an older child. By participating, they feel helpful and can rid themselves of some of the anxiety and possible jealousy they are beginning to feel.

One friend told us: "Our kids were so excited about having a new brother. But only after we started getting toys and clothes together did they realize the child would be living here. That dampened their spirits a bit, but they were quickly brightened by helping us paint the room and shop – they knew we wanted them to be part of the adoption."

Your child's ambivalence is normal and natural; any youngster feels upheaval and a loss of equanimity when there is to be an addition. It isn't because of adoption!

Once the sex of the new child is known – and most adoptive parents do know prior to placement – refer to him or her as "brother" or "sister," not "adopted brother" or "sister we're adopting." The adjective will unnecessarily make the child seem different from everyone else. Letting people (the children included) know you're comfortable with adoption makes them comfortable.

All small children, once they realize the baby is there to stay, have times of jealousy when they let their parents know it should go back to wherever it came from. Older children feel this way sometimes too, although they may not say so outright. They're better able to discuss or hide their feelings.

The sibling of an adopted child has an advantage in his own mind over the sibling of a new biological child. He has a place to send the new arrival! Therefore, don't be surprised if, while your new child is crying one day, your biological child sidles up to you and says: "I know why the baby's crying! He misses his mother!" Don't be hurt, either. You don't want your child to suppress or harbor his feelings. Sibling rivalry is normal and parents need not feel guilty or make their children feel guilty about it. Everyone needs time to adjust to new people and new situations. This is an excellent opportunity to take your older one on a lap for a hug, reassure him that it takes time to love new people, and explain that the new brother or sister is here to stay.

A child's reaction to a newly adopted sibling is much more likely to be affected by the fact that he has a new sibling than it is by the adoption. Our John has now lived through the arrival of two siblings, one adopted and one homegrown. John knew there was no other mother to return his little brother (homegrown) to, but he did suggest that "granny" might like the baby since she didn't have any!

Questions and comments continue for months, even years. They should be fielded as they come along. You might also want to ask your children from time to time if they want to discuss adoption. Let them learn that it is all right to mention the subject, as they, themselves, will sometimes have heard reactions of others that might make them feel that the subject is taboo. An example is the person who comes by and says: "You don't discuss the A-D-O-P-T-I-O-N with the others, do you?" (in front of an eight-year-old who can spell). Or the person who just says: "Well, you won't tell the others he's adopted, will you?" The important thing is to reassure the children, not to spare the feelings of the uninformed adults. The answer might be: "Of course the children know about adoption. Just like they know where babies come from. There's no reason not to know." (The answer ought to be given within earshot of as many children as possible!) If necessary, it can be referred to again later by simply saying to the children: "I guess Mrs. Jones just doesn't know about adoption, does she?"

A child may someday say: "But he's not my *real* brother." And he may add: "He came from another mommy and daddy." The instinctive response might be to say: "Yes, but she didn't want him, so they gave the baby to the agency to give to us to love." Although it might stop questions temporarily, it is a poor response. It opens the very definite possibility that if little brother acts up, we can just get rid of him too! But, it also leaves the possibility, especially if the sibling was adopted as a toddler or older, that if big brother or sister doesn't toe the mark, he or she might be next to go.

In these discussions, the love of the biological mother for the child should not be open to question. Nine times out of ten, it is an extremely difficult decision for a girl to give up her baby, and as the adopted child grows, he will know this. So, too, should the other siblings.

A good response is: "Not coming from Mommy's tummy doesn't mean he isn't a *real* brother. Being part of our family, now and always, is what makes him a *real* brother." It might be taken a step further if the child is old enough: "Daddy's my real husband, and I am his real wife, but we didn't come from the same mommy. Instead, when we married, the law said that we were a *real* husband and wife. Now we've adopted Tommy. He didn't come from my tummy, but the law says that he is our real son and your real brother."

Some children may press on. One mother told us her daughter said, "I know he's real. But he's not really real!" All you can do then is let the children know, by your words and actions, that adoption and birth are equally acceptable ways of having a brother or sister and that feelings don't depend on how the family came together.

Once the new adopted child is in the home, the old-timer will be telling the neighborhood and the world in general: "I have a new little sister at my house." Most children will ask eagerly to see the new addition or at least want a description. This makes big brother feel important, as he is spreading the word among his peer group, just as his parents do with theirs.

Every so often, however, he will come across the child

who says, "You can't have a new baby. Your mother wasn't pregnant." The sibling will say that the baby was adopted and then, most likely, take some sort of verbal barrage from the other child, who does not understand this new concept. There are three ways you can find out about this. First, the friend may be marched to the doorstep to see the new brother or sister and verify its membership in the family. Second, the sibling may mention the incident sometime after the fact. Third, the mother (or teacher) of the other child will call to apologize for his actions, and then say that she would explain it to him, but doesn't really know how.

You're now faced with the problem of discussing adoption with unrelated children, especially if the outside child is at your house. Once again, honesty and simplicity are the guidelines: "Our new child is a brother (or sister) for Johnny. We adopted him. There are two ways for children to come into a family . . ." The friend will be very curious, especially if he is older. He might ask why the child was adopted. You should say that adoption was your choice at the time. Introduce him to the new brother or sister, and offer a cookie from the cookie jar and time to stay and play. The adopted child should be accepted thereafter as "Johnny's new brother" (or sister).

The attitudes of neighborhood children and peers of siblings toward adoption will be affected by how their parents and siblings as well act toward the adopted child. If the mother of the neighbor or friend is involved in your adoption discussion with her child, or at least told about it, she will be better able to answer further questions and give perceptive explanations. Most people today do not regard adoption as unusual, but they might have difficulty talking about it. Time taken to discuss it with them will let them know how totally the parent accepts adoption.

A parent or teacher should not be overly sensitive if adoption becomes a dominant part of a sibling's – or adopted child's – play for a period of time. We have heard a story of one child who played "adopted baby" with her friends for several weeks. The parents let it go for a while, but then became somewhat concerned. The mother approached her daughter and asked why she was playing this way. The reply: "We always play with the mommy having the baby. We thought this would be fun, too, because there are two ways to have a baby in a family." She had learned her lesson well, and there was no reason for concern.

In family life, there are always times when one child is favored over another for some reason. This may cause indignant questions like, "How come he always gets dessert without eating his carrots? Do you love him more because he's adopted?" Or, "Does she get to watch TV because she's adopted and you give her more privileges?"

Most children know that they are loved but need reassurance from time to time. The above questions probably will never be asked in a family where a child is adopted as a baby, but when an older child is adopted, feelings may be quite strong in the siblings for a long period of time. Explanation and patience may help as parents try to ease the transition for a new child.

There will be times when special attention to the new child or baby is necessary. If the others know this in advance, it will be easier for them, as well. They, too, may require extra love and affection and special privileges.

Occasionally children may ask, "Weren't we good enough? Why do you need more kids?"

The answer may be: "Of course we love you very much. Because we are so pleased with you, and how you are growing, we want another child. We have lots of love to share, and this is another reason we want a child now. Sometimes in the beginning it will be hard for you, but anytime you need extra love and hugging, we have plenty to share. Your new brother doesn't mean less love for you."

It is possible that siblings might not care for the new child as a person. While the social worker may be of help in the "settling-in process" – which can take many, many months – it is the parents' prime responsibility to react to the needs of the biological children. Common interests of the children should be stressed and encouraged. If the biological child is older, he can teach games or help care for the younger one. But bear in mind that too much sharing too soon can cause a child's sense of balance and fair play to snap. This doesn't mean they're selfish – only that they are kids.

A vacation is a good way of beginning the new relationship for the family with children, particularly in the case of the adoption of an older child. All the family members will be able to relax and enjoy one another and the children can become acquainted in a relatively low-pressure atmosphere. Likes and dislikes will become apparent in many cases before toy or room sharing is necessary. Often a genuine affection will develop which will make life back home much simpler for all.

Children are really wonderful. They face life openly and can learn from each new experience. The advent of new siblings, no matter what the source, requires a period of adjustment on the part of an old-timer. It may be easy, especially if the adopted child is a baby, or it may be long and drawn-out. A child who is a friend, neighbor, or relative of an adopted child can learn more about family structure and meaning just from contact with the adoptive family. Let's hope that the adults who teach children about adoption are as open and accepting as the children themselves.

6/ Relatives and the Community

Adoption has not always been openly discussed. In the past, it was whispered about, so children might not know they had been adopted. Now, with the shortage of babies, controversial court cases, and the adoption of formerly "unadoptable" children, it has become a popular media issue.

More and more neighbors, friends and relatives who have been silent now seem to be coming out of the woodwork to discuss adoption with those of us who have increased our families in this way. In addition, there are countless others who do not necessarily want to discuss adoption, but have choice comments to insert into conversations.

It is important to respond and relate to these people, to show interest in their thoughts, and to help with misconceptions they might harbor. It also helps parents to deal with any feelings they themselves may have that adoption is "different," and helps them to feel comfortable when the subject is brought up. How those in the community think and feel about a particular family affects the ability of each family to thrive.

Lack of information or misinformation is the usual cause of negative remarks. Few persons are intentionally malicious. Fear of the unknown or untried causes people to safely retreat into their own little cocoons. Rather than learn about the new experience – in this case adoption – they instead are likely to make unfortunate remarks. These range from the absurd: "Oh, we think adoption is strange. There's something wrong with people who do it" to these more frequently heard statements:

"Adopted children are different."

"Do you treat him like you'd treat your own?"

"She's so lucky to have you for parents."

"What's your baby's last name?"

"I don't care what you say, these kids just aren't the same."

"I don't know what would make someone want to adopt a mixed kid."

"Anyone who adopts a child over six months needs his head examined. They're ruined for life by then."

"Sure you can love them when they're cute babies, but it's different when they're bigger."

"It's wonderful there are people like you who can do something like that (adopt)."

"Sometimes we almost forget your kids are adopted."

"She's so good to those kids. You'd never know they weren't hers."

Why do people have these feelings toward adoption? Many are well-intentioned persons, and don't even realize their remarks are insulting and hurtful to others. Often these are people who, as children, were friends or cousins to someone who had been adopted. They were aware of the adoption, and also knew that the other child was not. Possessing this secret was, in itself, enough to make the other child "different." Hearing it mentioned, and telling others the secret, made the adoption "strange." It's easy to see how future attitudes grew from such misguided beginnings.

Understanding, however, does not make uninformed comments easier for parents to accept. When an adoptive or prospective adoptive parent has to deal with these remarks, he does not always know how to react. Some use anger as a weapon; others are silent, and try to ignore the comment. The stronger the listener's emotional attachment to the speaker (i.e., relatives and grandparents) the harder it can be to cope.

There is no single "correct" method of responding to a negative comment, but there are several approaches to the various situations. We find it most useful to quietly correct certain statements as they occur.

Example: "I can't tell which is your own, and which is adopted."

Response: "They're both my own. One came into our family by adoption, the other by birth."

Example: "Which is your natural child?"

Response: "All children are natural. If you mean which did we give birth to, it was our son."

In the beginning, we often let such comments pass, feeling that the remark was of little consequence, or knowing the person meant well. But good intentions can bring major consequences if overheard by a child who is old enough to understand what is being said.

Spoken with a smile, these responses can help re-pattern an uninformed idea of adoption. It can be a positive learning experience for all involved.

There is *no* good reason not to respond, even to a shopkeeper selling you birth announcements!

Some families use stronger comments. It is for each person to decide how he/she is most comfortable facing a situation.

Example: "Aren't you wonderful to adopt a child like that!"

Response 1: "All children are entitled to parents, and we wanted a child, so we decided to adopt one at this time. We did it because we wanted to love a child, not to be wonderful."

Response 2: "We needed him as much as he needed us. It has nothing to do with being wonderful."

An adoptive parent should bear in mind that insulting someone will only reinforce his negative feelings. Instead, give him something to think about! Anger and hostile remarks won't change or modify his viewpoint toward adoption.

It is useful to ask a person why he feels as he does about adoption. Often there is a story from the past, as we have suggested. Listen! A parent should respond sympathetically to such a reminiscence. It will go a long way toward removing built-in prejudices.

Listening to a reminiscence of an adopted child who was "different," it is wise to bear in mind that such children, through no fault of their own, actually were treated in a special, but negative, way.

There are children who were not told of their adoption, and who found out through inappropriate sources.

There are children who were treated as objects who were bought.

There are children who, even by their parents, were labeled "adopted" ("my adopted daughter June") throughout childhood.

There are children who were treated as less than normal because their parents were unwed ("bad blood").

Although we cannot change the past for these children, we can change the present and future for our children, by helping friends, neighbors, and relatives to look at adoption in a new and different way. Always, an adoptive parent's own family and positive experiences are the best examples for showing others that adoption is a natural way to have a family.

One particular pet peeve of ours is the expression "natural mother," or "natural family." Social workers and adoptive parents are as likely to use it as anyone else. But the word "natural" connotes something that is good, proper or inherent, as opposed to "unnatural" – or perhaps "adopted." As long as persons say "natural parents" in contrast to "adoptive parents," they are making a qualitative judgment, even if they don't intend it. Instead, use "biological parent" and "adoptive parent." Good relationships make a family natural, no matter how it was put together.

Whether on a commuter train or at a neighborhood coffee party, parents should talk about adoption, as others share birth experiences. Each is a most exciting process! While each experience is personal, there are aspects of both to share with friends.

Our family has many favorite stories about our children. One concerns John's birth. For five consecutive days, his daddy forgot to bring the baby clothes to the hospital. At last it was time to go home, and baby John was wheeled into the room to be dressed to leave for home. You guessed – Daddy had forgotten the clothes once again, and John went back to the nursery as Daddy made a trip from Boston to Cambridge for the clothes he left at the front door. Mommy was quite annoyed.

We also remember when Jennifer came. Several children at John's kindergarten confronted him one day soon after her arrival and asked where his mommy had gotten the baby. John said, "She's my new sister," and one child piped up, "She can't be. Your mother wasn't pregnant. Anyone knows only pregnant people have babies." John then set him straight!

Each event was caused by the way a child came into our family. Each is a nice story to share with friends.

When pre-adoptive or adoptive parents have to deal with their relatives, the problems can at times be complex. Whether negative or positive, personal feelings in a family are often very strong. It is one thing to turn your back on a neighbor, quite another to tell your parent or your brother to mind his own business.

It is usually wise to let relatives know about an impending adoption in advance. Children are not possessions or objects, and any temptation to "surprise" a grandmother with a baby one day should be overcome. Chances are there will only be happiness and joy about the new arrival. But some grandparents (or sister, aunts, etc.) are not pleased about adoption, especially if a hard-to-place child is involved. The same person who says, "Isn't it nice Mr. and Mrs. Jones adopted a little black baby?" is quite disturbed to find that a little black baby is coming into her own family. This is one important reason for telling relatives early about adoption. Many possible problems can be worked out in advance. Others may not be successfully resolved at this time, but at least families should try to come to a workable solution.

For example, if one set of grandparents is opposed to the adoption, the husband and wife can discuss their feelings with one another and the parents. If no agreement about adoption is worked out, the husband and wife should come to an understanding about their relationships with the relatives in question once their child has arrived. Often fewer visits and telephone calls may be the result; rarely is the relationship unpleasantly halted for a period of time.

However, if a couple adopts, and finds that certain relatives make visiting hard and stressful, it may be best for the family to curtail the visits for a while.

Many families have found initial negative reactions from relatives when a transracial adoption is involved. It is exceedingly difficult, particularly for older people, to face their own latent feelings of racism. But families are often surprised to find that the relatives will gradually become accepting, even though the process may take many years. In the end, it is worth the wait. The family should try to be understanding and never turn away a first step at reconciliation by a relative. Even if it takes two years for a birthday to be remembered and recognized, at least they're trying.

Relatives at times may outwardly act pleased, but not inwardly adjust to adoption. No matter how positive the initial reaction seems to be, talk about the adoption anyway. It's an excellent way of uncovering latent feelings.

Favoritism may be a problem, particularly with grandparents. A biological child may receive more or better presents than an adopted one. When present-giving involves cousins, favoritism may not be as noticeable, but when both children are in one family, a difficult situation can arise. The children themselves are often aware of the difference.

Let the offending gift-giver know your feelings. It is important to resist any temptations to ignore favoritism because parents don't want to deprive one child of his treats, and they may hope to compensate at home to the other. Once relatives realize that a family considers each child as important as the others, they will probably fall into line.

What if the relatives ask for details of the adoption? They will undoubtedly ask what the parents know of the background of the baby. Religion, circumstances of birth, national origin, age of the biological parents – no nitty-gritty facts will be spared. Some people will share this information with relatives, or anyone else, for that matter. In general, however, we don't feel this is necessary. It can be very hurtful when an aunt says, "I want you to meet my adopted niece – she's French." We have developed a standard answer in our household, one in which we believe. "She's a Klibanoff" is the answer to all inquiries whether from friends or relatives because, after all, she is! Anything else we know is only for her when she grows up.

Every family has its own specific manner of living, but we summarize a few rules that will help all families.

1. Don't point out or accentuate the adoption. Labeling your own child "adopted" in every other breath is an open invitation to others to do the same.

2. However, don't try to hide the fact of adoption from others. It is nothing to be ashamed of. Even if the child does not know, someone else does, and will someday offer the information. Birth certificates and family documents often hold proof to origins, too. If a parent tells his child first, he doesn't have to worry about what others might say.

3. Always make it known, if the situation warrants, that your adopted child is to be treated like all the others, not as a "special" person.

4. Don't let an offensive remark on adoption pass by, no matter how insignificant it seems. Only by letting other people know the problem lies within them, will old-fashioned prejudices about adoption be removed.

We have addressed our remarks in this chapter to adoptive parents, because their interests and those of their families are most affected by what others think. As spokesmen for children, parents may have to protect their young from an often ignorant world. But what we say certainly isn't limited to adoptive parents. As long as adoption is part of our society, people are going to have to deal with it in their daily lives. If you've been guilty of thinking of adults or children who were adopted as different – whether or not you admit it – be willing to learn about the subject, and be more open-minded and thoughtful to others in the future.

HOW ADOPTION HAPPENS

7/ The Biological Mother and Father

THE person who sets the adoption process in motion is often given very little thought—at least by the adoptive parents. That person is the child's biological mother, usually an unwed mother.

There are many reasons why she is so overlooked. Some parents want to forget the fact that she ever existed. They consider her irresponsible or worthless. Some are embarrassed by the fact that she is the reason for their having children. Others hope that if she is never mentioned, the children might put off their questions about her. Most have never met a girl in the position of giving up a child, and just don't know what to think about her. No matter what the reason, it is time to discuss the unwed mother openly and give her the attention she deserves. In a previous chapter, we spoke about what to tell a child about his mother. In this chapter we consider her as an individual human being.

You must sometimes wonder about your child's first

mother. What did she look like? What did she think? Does she think about the baby, or you? These questions are natural. And while a family may never know the specifics about their child's first mother, or may know just a few details, maybe this will tell you something about her as a person.

We have talked with many girls who were single and about to deliver a child. Some of these girls we met at group meetings at a nearby home for girls who are single and pregnant. Here is a summary of our experiences in the form of one visit.

The immediate impression of the Home is of a college or boarding-school dormitory. There are girls in curlers, and girls shuffling around in housecoats and slippers. Some are plopped in front of a television, some are talking or whispering, others are munching sandwiches or drinking from paper cups. Virtually the only noticeable difference is that every one of these girls is from six to nine months pregnant.

You stand there and study their faces. The age range is wide, from about fourteen to the early twenties. There are more very young girls present than there would have been a few years back. The availability of abortion has cut down on the number of older girls who carry through a pregnancy.

Their faces are the faces of teen-agers everywhere. They don't have hardened looks; they are not constantly teary-eyed or depressed. Once you begin to talk with them, you sense the deep concern they feel for their yet unborn children.

The discussion groups are small, four to six girls, a social worker, and two adoptive couples – one with only adopted children, the other with both adopted and biological. The purpose of the meetings is to help the girls plan for the future – for themselves and their children. Previously, the girls had met with other single girls who decided to keep their children. Keeping a baby has become an increasingly popular trend, and the girls are aware of it. Now they want to meet the people who might adopt and raise their children, if they decide to surrender them.

The girls tease each other about their diets, and the fact that some can use only skimmed milk in their coffee because of a recent gain in weight. They joke and ask us to guess which girl is overdue, and which is about to have twins. By the time the coffee ritual is finished, we are all on a first-name basis and know a little about one another.

The worker has asked for questions from the girls at a previous meeting and has written them down on small cards in anticipation of silent moments. However, as in all groups of girls, there is at least one talkative one and she starts things off. Not surprisingly, she has usually pretty much decided to place her child for adoption and has the personal concern which drives her to ask her questions. But all the girls want to know the answers. Here are some of the questions we were asked (and some of our replies).

Q. "Do you love your adopted child as much as your biological one? Do you treat them the same?"

A. "We love both of our children. Once they come into our house, either by 'home growing' or adoption, they become ours. We don't differentiate them according to how we had them, but we do treat them as individuals, according to age, personality and interests."

Q. "What do you tell your biological child about adoption?"

A. "We say that there are two ways to have children in a family, adoption and reproduction. We chose to have one child one way and the second another way."

Q. "Won't he resent the baby? Feel it doesn't belong?"

A. "Most children have sisters and brothers, so giving up the spot of 'king pin' is something he's witnessed before in other families, and something he would have to do no matter where the baby came from. We tell him that it is because we love him so much that we want more children. We have a lot of love to share, and adding to the family doesn't take love from him. It's natural for him to test our feelings. What four-year-old wouldn't want at some time or another to get rid of the new arrival?

"John has asked upon occasion if we're always going to keep Jennifer – usually when she's getting all the attention. But his feelings aren't because she's adopted. The little boy across the street (he's John's age) had a brother by birth. When the brother annoyed him, he would suggest that he be given to the milkman for a quarter."

Q. "What will you say about me?"
(The girls ask this because they are very concerned that we not think of them as "cheap" or "tramps." Often, this is a reaction to the response of family and neighbors. Though their self-esteem may be low because of the untimely pregnancy, all are proud of the decision to have the baby. For them, abortion would have made a mistake much worse.)

A. "We will say that we respect you for making a difficult decision, one that affects your life and the life of the baby. You decided to place him or her for adoption because this is what you feel will be best for the baby's future. We want you to know, too, that on birthdays and other special occasions, many adoptive parents think about you, the child's first mother, and the fact that you may be thinking of the child and how proud you would be."

Q. "What about religion? Will you bring my child up in your religion?"

A. "The child is a member of our family and no differentiation among our family is made for religion."

Q. "Will you send your children to college?"
(As the evening goes on, it becomes more and more apparent that, like any other mother, these girls want the best possible for their children. Because most of the girls are young and often not from wealthy homes, where access to abortion would prevent them from missing school, most think of higher education as something they are unlikely to obtain.)

A. "Our children will all be given as much opportunity for education as possible. If we can afford it and if the children show the inclination and interest, we will, of course, send them to college. However, if their aptitudes and interests point in another direction, we will help them in those other fields also."

Q. "What about birth control? What if your daughter gets pregnant?"

A. "We will discuss sex and birth control with our children as they grow. If our child feels the need for birth control, we will help him or her to obtain it. We only hope our children will come to us to discuss it. If our daughter becomes pregnant, we will stick by her no matter whether she has an abortion or gives birth, and we will give her all the support we can."

The questions go on. "Will you spank your children?" "What if they lie?" "What would you do if they didn't want to go to school?" "What if they get into fights?"

The girls are seeking several things through their questions.

They want to be sure that adoptive families will love "their" children and not favor a biological child to an adopted one. They have the same myths and doubts about adoption that much of the public has, so their questions stem from curiosity and lack of knowledge as well as personal interest.

Many unwed mothers have troubled family histories. They've been physically or mentally abused in the past. At the age of fourteen, they may no longer be wanted by their own families. Some have nowhere to go after the baby is born. These girls are searching for a home and family for themselves as much as for the babies. Their questions reflect what they would have wanted, and nothing but the best will be good enough for their children.

Most of all, these girls are searching for love. Many of them have none, and they want it for their babies. What is more pathetic than a fifteen-year-old girl with a six-day-old baby who has no place to go? Her family won't take her in, and there is no foster family who will take both her and the baby. It is very simple to say that the easiest and best solution is to place the child for adoption and put the girl in a foster home where she might find some affection and have a chance to grow up herself. But, it is also easy to understand why she might desperately cling to the infant, and consider it her only chance in life – all that she has to love in the world.

Not all adopted children are borne by unwed mothers. There are several other ways children come to need homes. Sickness and death sometimes leave children without a family. Such family tragedy is the source of many sibling groups and older children. Child abuse and neglect often cause the courts to remove a child permanently from a home. Some married women who give birth to children of men other than their own husbands place these children for adoption. The unwed mother, however, remains the source for over 80 percent of children who are adopted by persons unrelated to them and over 60 percent of all adopted children.[1]

The changing social climate, including the movement for women's liberation, has resulted in more and more single women keeping their babies. Since 1970 the percentage of out-of-wedlock children who are adopted has been decreasing slightly.[2] Many agencies are finding, however, that the mothers sometimes surrender the children when they become toddlers, when the novelty of having a new "toy" begins to wear off and the added responsibility and commitment becomes real. The mother is more tied down and shut off from her friends and other young people because of the child's need for care. She may consider placing the child in foster care while she makes life plans for herself. A desire to return to school or to marry, or annoyance at the way grandparents have taken over the child can cause her to reconsider her decision to raise the child. Sometimes parents who adopt these children are bitter that the child has been unnecessarily prevented from having a full family life starting on Day One. This may well be unfortunate. But the parents should also appreciate the amount of courage it took finally to reach a solution for both mother and child that might help both to reach fuller potential as people with separate lives than they would have reached together.

Parents should remember, too, that adoption may not always be the best solution. There are more and more unwed mothers who are able successfully to keep a baby and provide loving and responsible parental care. Although adoption is the subject of this book and the means by which many children find families, it is only one option for the unwed mother and her child. For some mothers, keeping and raising the baby is not only a possibility, but the best long-range plan. For others, particularly younger girls, legal abortion might be the proper alternative.

While biological mothers have been given little thought, the biological fathers (unflatteringly referred to as the "putative" fathers by most social workers and law professors) have been universally ignored. Some agencies now have fathers take part in meetings and interviews and try to help them as well as the mothers, but much more is left to be done.

The general public seems to believe that babies who are placed for adoption come from "hit-and-run" fathers. As some people say: "If they were 'decent' people, they would marry the mother."

Many times the fathers would have married the mothers, but parental interference, young age, or a mutual decision to wait and see what might develop has prevailed. This doesn't mean the father has lost interest. Nor does it mean the father lacks feelings. Boyfriends often make visits to a maternity home while awaiting the birth of the baby. One father we knew sat in the waiting room of a hospital while his girlfriend gave birth; he paced the floor like any other expectant male.

For the most part, however, these men have been denied professional counseling. Workers are quick to say that if the father is "known" (the term reflecting a bias in itself), he is encouraged to come in and discuss the situation. However, if a social welfare agency is a rather imposing place for the mother, it is even more threatening to the father.

Fathers have feelings and emotional needs, too. They do not carry the baby, but they are not insensitive, either. In order to help them emotionally cope with the pregnancy, the problems they may be encountering at home or school, and in order to help them mature after the experience, social agencies should work with them as well. Responsibility is not encouraged when the father is intentionally left out of the process of working through this difficult human problem. Counseling groups intended for fathers of children born out of wedlock, both before and after the birth, and including the mother, would be worthwhile agency projects. The legal profession is beginning to broaden its recognition of the interests of the fathers; the social work profession and the general public should keep pace.

8/ Adoption through an Agency

Many people believe the myths that adoption agencies are filled with maiden ladies who smile sweetly and hand bright little babies to childless couples. These little old ladies are also said to have some evil lurking behind their cooperative exterior by searching relentlessly behind furniture and under rugs for dust and grime, and appearing out of nowhere to check up on the adoptive family. If the family passes inspection, the worker will pick and choose among the rooms full of orphans to find just the right one for the family. If the parents are tall and redheaded, the child will be too. If a redhead isn't available, the family need only wait around till one comes up. Then off they go, Mommy and Daddy and Baby, into Never-Never-Land.

The reality is quite different. In the first place, adoption is usually only one service of a child welfare agency. Although in the past it may have been a main function, changes in the needs of our society are bringing about changes in agencies to keep pace with today's world.

Child welfare agencies were established around the turn of the century to provide care for abandoned or neglected children. They not only housed children in foster care and orphanages, but found families for them through adoption. Traditionally, these were white middle- and upper-class families for white babies. The children who now need homes are older and mixed-racial and children with special needs; the families come from all walks of life. Homes are not just for the rich and the white!

The agency provides many services. The unwed mother is given counseling about her future decision for her baby: to place it for adoption or to keep it. She is given medical care, and the agency will help her find a place to live if she needs it. Although the orphanages of fable no longer exist, agencies do employ foster families who take care of babies and children until they have permanent homes. Sometimes these foster families will keep the children for prolonged periods, often several years, if families can't be found for them. If a child cannot function in a home setting, or if the agency has no appropriate foster parents, children can be placed in group settings, often under agency sponsorship. All the adoption services are also rendered. These include recruitment of prospective parents, the "home study," placement of the child, follow-up care and preparation of all reports and papers necessary for court proceedings.

Is there a conflict of interest in serving both the biological mother and adoptive families? In the past there may have been attempts by some workers to persuade a girl to place her child for adoption, but this kind of unprofessional behavior is unlikely today. Both society and social workers are more accepting in their attitudes toward unwed motherhood. Also, the counseling and adoption services are usually provided by different workers. Thus, each worker can concentrate fully on the needs of his particular client, and not worry about anyone else.

Who are the social workers? Social work has been a middle-class profession, and adoption workers were the élite of the group. It wasn't a particularly hard life, deciding which baby to place in which family. Social workers would choose among many prospective adoptive parents to find the ones which best fitted their conception of an ideal family. Older couples, those with low income, and those of mixed religion were easily rejected, often with little or no cause. Agency policy on the types of people they wished to serve – for both unwed mothers and prospective adoptive parents – discriminated against the poor and the minority races and religions.

Adoption and family service agencies have to be flexible enough to consider as individuals each family and each person they work with. They will then best serve the children who now wait to come into families by adoption.

Adoption agencies are now attempting to serve the needs of the entire community better. More and more social workers from minority groups are being hired. And graduate schools in social work are opening their doors to blacks, Spanish-speaking people and American Indians. Increasingly, the agency is becoming a professional resource available to give help to children and families whenever they need it.

As the agencies find themselves with fewer white babies, but not fewer families wanting children, the workers are faced with learning more about the children who need the homes, and how to help them get together with families. Many agencies are, for the first time, actively recruiting black and minority group adoptive families. A child who has special needs because of a mental or physical handicap, a child of one race being placed in a home of another, and an older child: all need to have more skills applied to their care and adoptive placement than does the healthy baby. Only by learning about the children they serve, and understanding the problems that may arise in adoptions, can the social workers adequately and successfully serve the community. This is one reason for the extra education many agencies now require, and for the courses many older workers seek out. One note of caution here – degrees in social work are well and good, but experience and feelings of appreciation for human beings are still the most important characteristics of the good social worker. One social worker said to us, "I hope you say nice things about us in your book." They should realize they are their own best (or worst) advertisement.

Why the change in numbers and types of available children? Certainly abortion is one reason. Fewer pregnancies being carried through to term mean fewer babies. In addition, infertile couples aren't the only ones who want to adopt children. Prospective parents choose formerly "hard-to-place" children simply because of a desire to love and provide a home for a child who needs one. Parents have formed groups to confront agencies with their requests for hard-to-place children and to talk about matters of mutual interest. Increased awareness and activity by adoptive parents have also led to reevaluation of the roles of both the agencies and the social workers.

As the formerly hard-to-place children are finding homes, the agencies too are beginning to diversify. One agency – the one we used – originally served just as a shelter for homeless children. As time went on, they placed white babies and toddlers in families. Eventually, in the mid-1960's, couples came to them requesting mixed-racial and American Indian children (due to publicity these groups had received). Slowly they began placing these children, and as they discovered that the adoptions were successful, they placed more and more of them. At the same time, there were fewer and fewer white babies available. As waiting lists grew to two and three years for these children, the agency started asking couples to consider the other children who needed homes. By 1970 there were so few babies available for adoption that the agency felt that it was necessary to stop placing white newborn children and concentrate its energies on other children who were already born. In addition to the babies of other races, this meant the other children who lived in the residential care facilities which the agency had maintained throughout its existence. These children were all over five years of age, and all had some degree of emotional difficulty.

By 1971, the baby shortage – white, black, and mixed-racial – had struck all the agencies in Greater Boston. As a result, the agency decided to devote its energies strictly to older children and the children in their custody – the ones most in need of families at this time.

There is an urgent need now for homes for older and mixed-racial children, sibling groups, and emotionally, physically handicapped, and retarded children. In addition, the abused child and the war orphan need a family, as do thousands of children who are waiting for short- or long-term foster families. Social welfare agencies are faced with different – and more difficult – challenges today from any they have ever had.

Chapter 3 has explained what a family does when they consider adopting through an agency. Several things can happen as a result of the first agency contact. Some agencies invite all callers to a group meeting, at which that agency's policies and procedures are discussed. Some will make an appointment with one couple at a time. Many agencies ask the caller what type of child he is interested in, may say there are no white babies available, but may welcome the couple to come and hear about the children who are waiting for homes. Others will refer a couple to an agency which might be more suited to a particular request (a specific religion might be such a request), or just ask a couple to remain on a waiting list for an indefinite period of time. A number of agencies say, "No, there are no babies available. Call back next year."

We believe this last response is an abdication of the agency's public responsibility. All prospective parents should be given the courtesy of having the agency services explained to them, and then given the option of being placed on a waiting list. If a parent is told it may be several years, but wishes to wait, the agency should honor the request. It is unfair and unnecessary to kill all hope.

To be sure, the couple who wants the white, healthy baby has to realize their chances may be extremely slim.

We ask all couples looking for this particular type of baby to think at least about the children already waiting for homes.

Assume that a family has seen the agency, and filled in the application forms. What happens next? Once again, policy varies from agency to agency. Some make a home study immediately and ask the couple, if accepted, to wait till a child is available. Since unexpected pregnancy, job transfers and other events can prevent completion of an adoption, this is not the ideal procedure. Rather, many agencies ask families to wait a certain length of time until the home study is begun; after that the time before placement is fairly short. During the delay before the study, the agency may reassure the couple by telephone calls or letters that they are not forgotten. A few agencies are beginning to conduct group studies, with several families and usually more than one worker. This is good for several reasons. First, it removes the onus from one social worker of having to play God in each decision. Second, it gives the couple the benefit of being with other couples in a similar situation. Third, everyone can learn from the group experience, especially when it is relaxed and non-judgmental.

The nature of the home study often depends on the agency, or even the social worker, conducting it. Traditionally, they have consisted of several interviews between a worker and the couple, some with husband and wife together, some with each separately. If the family has children, they may also be interviewed. The home is often – but not always – visited.

We were living in a five-room apartment when we adopted. When the worker at our group meeting emphasized that the family shouldn't overclean for the social worker's home visit, she mentioned visiting homes where there were two or three children, but not even any toys in sight. Everything was in closets or on shelves. Everybody chuckled and agreed it was silly to work so hard for a social worker's visit. Nevertheless, when Miss James called to arrange her visit at our home, we put in several days of scrubbing and cleaning "just in case." The afternoon of the great visit finally arrived, and Miss James called to say she couldn't arrange to get a car to visit us. We lived rather far from the agency, and there was no easy public transportation to our house, so she suggested we bring John there to see her. We were so disappointed, after all our work, that we drove into Boston and brought her out to the house ourselves!

Prospective adoptive parents are almost universally concerned about how to respond to the social worker's questions. Each family wants to present a picture of the ideal marriage and homelife, and some practice responses to likely questions beforehand. There are even books that give advice on how to talk with the worker. But each family and each social worker is different. Since no two situations can ever be the same, it is difficult to generalize about how – or whether – to prepare in advance for the experience. When we adopted, our worker felt, for example, that the child's religious upbringing was not of major significance, yet friends who adopted from the same agency two years later ran into considerable problems with their worker. They were told that religion was of prime importance in adoption, and that the judge would ask at the finalization whether or not they had followed their religion in the year after placement. This couple had trouble communicating with their worker and the worker had difficulty getting her role straight.

One of the major problems prospective parents have with agency adoption is confusion over what the agency is trying to accomplish. Does the worker play God? To some extent the answer has been and still is yes. Too often workers set up ideal images for families, approve those who most nearly fit them and reject those who don't. This has led to rejection for reasons such as lack of income, certain religious preferences, physical problems or certain chronic medical diseases. To most couples these seem arbitrary and unnecessary.

There is no doubt that there are some couples who shouldn't adopt and others who ought not to do so at the time they have picked. All judgment cannot be eliminated in an adoption. But there is no need for agencies to project Godlike images. Group interviews may be helpful in changing that image. Several couples going through the process with two or more workers removes the burden from one worker having to make decisions alone. Conflicts of personality are less likely, and the parents hear several individual viewpoints put forth.

Perceptive social workers with experience and understanding can be of valuable help to prospective adoptive parents in dealing with their attitudes about adoption, their approach to child-rearing, and their relationship with one another. The proper role of an agency should *not* be to predict which people would make the "best" adoptive parents. Rather, the agency's role should be *to help those who want children to become successful in the demanding job of parenting.*

The approval or rejection of parents by agencies has serious consequences. If agencies continue to conceive of their role in a self-righteous and patronizing manner, they will exacerbate already serious social problems and provoke greater governmental regulation. If exercised unreasonably, the agency's power can be one of the major causes of independent and even black-market adoptions. Fear of being turned away may drive a desperate couple toward illegal means and unscrupulous persons. Actual rejection, especially when insensitively or arbitrarily handled, is even more likely to do so. Agencies must re-examine their reasons for rejecting a family. They must be more willing to discuss rejection with the family. Many people have contacted adoptive parents' groups to say that they were turned down, but no reason was given – it was "classified" information. How degrading! How totally callous to the fact that human beings are being treated like objects! Any family rejected is entitled to the reasons and to consultation with the chief caseworker. Further, they should be worked with to overcome any problems that are deemed serious. No one should ever be flatly turned away.

If the prospective adoptive couple has completed the home study and been accepted, the next step is the arrival of the child. It can occur within days for older or hard-to-place children, or, given the recent small supply of babies, many months later. If a baby is being placed, the usual process is for the couple to come to the agency or some other relatively private place and receive the child. Some agencies which do not have nursery facilities for babies have been known to bring couples their baby in a park or even at a shopping center parking lot. Sometimes, the child is brought directly to the parents' home.

Contact with the agency after placement varies. A worker will likely make home visits just to see how everything is going. The older the child, and the more specialized the adoption, the more important these visits are. Parents should feel free to discuss questions they may have; there is no penalty attached to them. Nor will a child who has ice cream on his shirt be repossessed.

Some agencies have group meetings after placement so that families can discuss their experiences with one another as well as a social worker. We have met couples who say they have no need for such a group, but it will usually be helpful to get together with families who have something in common, even if there is no apparent "need."

The last formal contact between the adopting parents and the agency usually takes place in court when the adoption is finalized. But this does not mean that the agency ceases to exist on that day. It is always there if a family needs its services or advice.

9/ Independent Adoption

Adoption sponsored by child welfare agencies is only part of the picture. Almost one quarter of the children adopted by persons unrelated to them are adopted without agency sponsorship. In addition, almost all of the adoptions by relatives of the children occur independent of an agency.[1] With the decrease in the number of infants available for adoption, the percentage of independent adoptions will continue to climb.

Independent adoption can occur in one of two ways: the biological parents and the adoptive parents may deal with one another directly, or they may act through an intermediary, usually a doctor or a lawyer.

Two states – Delaware and Connecticut – completely forbid independent adoptions; some, like Colorado, permit surrender of children only to licensed agencies; most of the rest require an agency investigation before an adoption can be legalized by a court, though they do not require that the child be placed in the adoptive family by an agency. In forty-eight of our states, therefore, independent adoption per se is not illegal.

We must take care to separate what is commonly called "black-market" adoption from most independent adoptions. An adoption is said to be "black-market" only when it involves a monetary reward for the person who places the child, above and beyond a reasonable fee for the legitimate services of any profession (medical, legal, for example) he might have. It is this fraction of independent adoptions that is most responsible for the confusion and unpleasant reputation common to all independent adoptions. Recent investigations by journalists indicate that it may be time for the courts, the bar associations, the medical societies and adoption agencies cooperatively to define, limit, and regulate reasonable professional fees.[2] The unscrupulous person who promotes a black-market adoption plays on the emotions of desperate people and is not likely to serve their best interests. The risks are very great.

Although no responsible authority justifies the type of profiteering in children represented by black-market adoption, there is disagreement and controversy about independent, as opposed to agency-sponsored, adoption.

From the point of view of the adoptive parents, there are certain risks in an independent adoption which are not as likely to be present in an agency-sponsored adoption. First, there is a greater chance of reinvolvement of the biological parent and the withdrawal of her consent. In cases where the circumstances of the surrender of the child are unknown, the adoptive parents risk the chance that the biological parents may not have acted with clear intent or may have been subject to fraud or duress – in other words, pressured into their decision – thereby jeopardizing the legal validity of the surrender. In cases where there was direct contact between biological and adoptive parents, the risk stems from the loss of anonymity. A 1963 study of independent adoption in Florida found that sometimes the biological parent insists on visiting the adoptive home and seeing the child. It documented cases where the visits were accompanied by emotional outbursts and pleas to have the child returned. Another problem experienced by adoptive families was the attempt by biological parents to extort money from them to let them keep the children. In one case, a mother tried to get the adoptive parents to take an older child of hers as well, as the price of keeping the one originally placed.[3]

Second, the adoptive parents usually have little or no knowledge of the medical history of the biological parents or of the child, or of the course of the pregnancy. Therefore, there is a greater chance that unexpected physical or mental disabilities could develop in the child.

Finally, without good legal advice, an independent adoption could result in legal conflict when the petition for adoption is brought to court for finalization. Most of the adoption cases which have resulted in legal battles requiring decisions by the highest state courts have involved independent placements.

Prospective adoptive parents who consider seeking a child from a source other than a licensed agency should, therefore, follow these rules.

1. Hire your own trusted, reputable lawyer who is capable of assuring that the entire process complies with

the relevant legal requirements in all states or countries involved in the adoption.

2. Deal only with an intermediary whose reputation and professionalism are above reproach and whose fee is reasonable and limited to the services of his profession – not for placing a child.

3. Discover as much as possible about the circumstances of the surrender of the child.

4. Discover as much as possible about any mental or physical problems the child might have and about the course of the pregnancy.

5. Arrange for a thorough evaluation of the child by medical specialists of your own choosing.

As for finding a reputable intermediary, the best reference is a parent who has adopted independently in the past. An adoptive parents' group should be able to identify one. Otherwise, spreading the word among doctors and lawyers in the community may uncover some good leads.

From society's point of view, independent adoption presents some special problems.[4] Since there is no review of the prospective adoptive family prior to placement, there is always the danger that the child will be neglected, abused, or otherwise improperly treated. This is true even in those states which require an agency investigation prior to granting of the final decree, because there is a lapse between the time when the child arrives and the time when the family goes to court to finalize the adoption. In addition, if the prospective parents decide at some point prior to final adoption that they do not want to go through with it, there may not be an agency ready and willing to step in and find an alternative home for the child. The following account of an independent adoption from the records of a United States Senate subcommittee illustrates these risks.

> . . . The prospective adoptive couple had had a great tragedy. Their 6-year-old boy had passed away, and they were anxious to receive a child who looked just like their 6-year-old boy.
>
> Mr. B [the intermediary] sent them to Augusta, Ga. The adoptive father in this case arrived one day in Georgia, and he was met at the airport by Miss Hamilton. She was with a boy who was about 6 years old. The adoptive father remained in town no more than an hour and a half, and he then returned to Los Angeles.
>
> He immediately rejected the boy, and after having him in his house for several months, passed him on to another couple in Los Angeles. The boy was then passed on to a third couple. At no time was he adopted. While in the hands of the third couple, he became so malicious and so maladjusted as a result of these repeated placements that he finally attempted to poison his third foster mother, and as a result he has had to be sent to an institution. . . .[5]

Had an agency been involved from the outset in this adoption, the tragic occurrences would most likely have been averted. The first prospective adoptive couple sought to replace a child who had died and were dissatisfied when their new son was not exactly like their deceased one. This type of motive would not be honored by an agency and there would never be an attempt precisely to match characteristics. Beyond that, the agency would have stepped in to protect the child after one unsuccessful placement.

Despite all the obvious risks, there still remains real doubt whether the most commonly suggested reform – exclusive agency placement – would be a wise course at the present time. The independent adoption can offer opportunities for both the biological parent and the prospective adoptive parent that may be foreclosed by agencies.

Not all unwed pregnant women need or want agency counseling. Some find the structure and authority of an agency threatening; others regard it as patronizing. Many prefer to relate to a trusted doctor, lawyer or minister, both for the assurance of a home for their child of which they would approve and for the quiet anonymity of the entire process. An often-heard complaint about sectarian agencies is the tendency of some to make the unwed mother feel guilty about her condition. Such practice harms the public image of all agencies and deters unmarried women from seeking agency services.

If the emotional, medical and other needs of today's unwed mothers-to-be can best be met by persons independent of child welfare agencies, then it would be cruel to make the acts of such persons illegal. Agencies ought to be viewed as in a competition with other professional and nonprofessional resources to serve the public. Only when their services are capable of meeting the real social needs will the argument for outlawing independent adoption be persuasive to the unmarried mother. The social work profession should begin to recognize that it does not have a monopoly on the ability to serve her needs.

Persons who want to adopt have often turned to independent adoption because of frustration with the process of agency adoption. Their frustration has been commonly caused by the restrictive and petty eligibility requirements of some agencies, which, in effect, exclude certain people from the opportunity to be a family to a child who needs one. Among such requirements are:

– that the religion of the adoptive parents match that of the biological mother;

– that people over a certain age may not adopt;

– that adopting parents must earn a certain minimum amount of income;

– that divorced or single people are unfit; or

– that people able to bear children are not eligible to adopt.

Couples in which one or both partners have been previously married and couples who have interfaith marriages have also been excluded by some agencies. Various kinds of physical and mental health problems often result in the rejection of a family. A 1966 study comparing couples adopting independently with those adopting through an agency found that in the independent group, there was a greater frequency of previous marriage, a higher proportion of Jewish couples and lower levels of occupation and education.[6]

What is particularly frustrating to prospective parents is the refusal of many agencies to give persuasive reasons for a rejection or to offer any realistic chance for reconsideration. The day may not be far off when the politicization of adoptive parents reaches a point where agencies are forced to establish a fair and open system of formal appeals and written standards for judgment, much like those required of governmental agencies which deny individual rights.

Certain arbitrary agency requirements are often defended on the basis that the small supply of adoptable children demands limits on who can adopt in order to give the most "suitable" parents (in the eyes of the social worker) a fair chance. The result of these restrictions, however, is to increase the demand for children through independent adoption and to damage the reputation of adoption agencies.

Despite the sometimes unfair and restrictive policies of agencies, many social workers argue that independent adoption should be outlawed. Such action would, in the first place, be difficult to enforce. Experience in Delaware and Connecticut indicates that black-market adoptions might increase, that couples might leave the state in order to adopt, or that families might for many years care for children they've found independently, without seeking a more permanent and secure relationship for the child through adoption.[7] Also, prohibiting independent adoption would rest on the dubious assumption that agencies are, indeed, able to pick the "best" parents. There is wide disagreement on whether agencies have any special expertise in this area at all. About all one can say with certainty is that social workers tend to agree among themselves on the factors that make for suitable couples: well-adjusted personalities; emotional maturity; a stable marital relationship; positive feelings about children; healthy feelings about childlessness; and an appropriate motivation for adopting.[8] Applying these general standards to particular people is not easy, however, and often a professional judgment is tinged by subjective or irrational criteria.

Recent evidence indicates nothing to support the theory of special agency expertise. The 1963 study of independent adoptions in Florida, mentioned above, was done ten years after placement. It showed that the percentage of unsatisfactory placements was about equal to those found in agency adoptions.[9] The study revealed that only 4 percent of the children adopted independently had any degree of physical or intellectual disability and only 7 percent of the families encountered problems from biological parents, and these usually ceased after the final decree of adoption was issued.[10]

A second study goes so far as to conclude that independent adopters showed fewer emotional problems than agency adopters, better marital adjustment and less conflict within their families.[11]

The argument against independent adoption which is based on the premise that agencies can predict a successful, permanent family relationship is not persuasive. When we consider, in addition, the failure of agencies to meet fully, fairly, and effectively the needs of both unwed mothers and prospective adoptive parents, we must conclude that for today's world, independent adoption is an important and necessary social instrument.

10/ Children in Foster Care

CHILDREN who are adopted at a very young age are the lucky ones. But they are only some of the many thousands of children who each year are orphaned, surrendered, abandoned, abused or neglected. Many of the others – more than 325,000 in any given year [1] – are wards of public and private agencies because their parents are unable, unwilling or unfit to care for them properly. Some of these children cannot easily live in a family or in their community and are sent, on a long-term basis, to various kinds of residential institutions – "reform" schools, institutions for the retarded and treatment centers for the emotionally disturbed. Most of them, however, are placed in foster care with a family.

Foster care is legally different from adoption. The foster parents have no legal rights or obligations to the children, and the children have no legal claim to rights or benefits from the foster parents. No names are changed, and the children have no inheritance rights. A social welfare agency is the legal guardian or custodian of the child on a "temporary" basis and acts as the parent, usually subject to a court order, but sometimes through a voluntary agreement with the biological parents. The relationship of the child to his biological parents or previous guardian is not ended, merely in abeyance.

Theoretically, foster care is supposed to provide care for children whose parents encounter a sudden crisis and can no longer function effectively as a family unit. Generally accepted reasons for placing a child in foster care are: a temporary crisis such as the critical illness of a parent; the inability of one parent to care for the child after the trauma of divorce, separation or desertion; short-term mental problems; physical or mental abuse of the child by the parent; and the exacerbation of a child's emotional disturbance by contact with his parents.[2] Theoretically, during the period of foster care, a child welfare agency is working to put the original family together again as quickly as possible.

That is the theory.

The reality is quite different.

In a very recent study of the six thousand children in family foster care in Massachusetts, it was found that most foster children stay in foster care for over three years.[3] A commission consisting of judges, social work professionals, lawyers and parents made the following conclusions based on that study: that despite the generally temporary purpose of foster home care in theory, it is more often than not a permanent status for the child; that foster children receive inadequate diagnostic, treatment and case management services; that biological parents are permitted to maintain parental rights without demonstration of significant interest in their children; and that foster children are not given sufficient opportunity for a permanent family through adoption.[4]

Other studies have shown that foster children are damaged children, fearful of further trauma, lacking in self-worth, distrustful, angry, longing to love yet fearing to love.[5] They have often been called "the orphans of the living."

Most of the so-called "hard-to-place" children come from foster homes. Those who remain there deserve to have permanent plans made for them. These usually mean either a return to their original family or adoption.

When a child enters foster care, he does so either because his parent and the agency have mutually agreed that he become a foster child, or, more commonly, because a court has separated him from his parents and awarded temporary legal custody or guardianship to the agency. Since foster care is considered a temporary legal relationship, the court assumes that the family will eventually be reunited. Before a foster child can be adopted, the rights of the biological parents must be terminated, either by voluntary consent or by a court order. There have been many administrative roadblocks and, at times, much conscious resistance, to finally terminating the rights of biological parents (see Chapter 16), but we hope the trend will be in the direction of honoring the rights of children to a permanent family rather than the claims of parents who demonstrate no real concern for their children. We do not believe that adoption is always the best plan for the child, but its proven success justifies a much greater effort than has been expended in the past to make it available to the children in long-term foster care.

Two new developments will hasten this movement. First, there are the new subsidy laws. Over ten states now permit public financial assistance for children who are adopted. One barrier to adoption of foster children has been the cost of care, especially for children with special needs and families with low incomes. Foster parents wishing to adopt these children formerly had to sacrifice this financial aid often crucial to the child's well-being. Adoption subsidies make possible permanent families for thousands of children otherwise "trapped" in foster care.

The second important development is the organization and politicization of foster parents. They have already brought pressure to bear on agencies to rethink the old rule that foster parents could not adopt their foster children. Based on the fear that previous contact with biological parents may handicap an adoption, this rule is gradually being relaxed, especially in those cases where there has been no such previous contact. Why remove a foster child from a loving relationship with foster parents to be adopted by strangers, when the foster parents want to adopt him?

We are often asked questions about foster care which don't directly relate to adoption. Here are a few of them and the answers we give.

How can I become a foster parent?

You should contact a public or private child welfare agency and the public departments responsible for youthful offenders, mental health, mental retardation and handicapped children. The requirements vary tremendously, depending on the job to be done, but the basic qualifications would be a commitment to the welfare of children, ability to be a responsible parent and the realization that foster parenthood is different from raising your own children.

While we stress the temporary nature of foster care, for some children long-term foster care may be preferable to adoption. This might include children whose parents are chronically ill or even in jail. The parent cannot physically care for his child in these cases, but the love on both sides, as well as some visiting, makes long-term foster care the best solution. But whether long-term or temporary, foster parents should be committed to doing all they can to help their foster children mature and grow in a warm, loving environment.

What is the proper role of the foster parent?

More and more, the foster parent is being called upon to be a treatment giver and advocate for the child. Today's foster children are coming from families with great disorganization and emotional problems. They are also coming from institutions for the retarded, disturbed and delinquent. The foster parent is not merely a source of care and protection. He or she is the central treatment resource. He or she is becoming a professional employee of an agency, whose pay and training should reflect his or her importance to the life of the child. Agencies will have to strengthen their efforts to recruit and support foster parents and, at the same time, be more willing to make decisions about the rights of biological parents which are based on the welfare of the child. From the outset, the foster parent should know whether the care he is to give is short-term or long-term and precisely how much "treatment" he is expected to make available to the child.

Do foster parents take children to earn money?

There is no doubt that, in the past, some people became foster parents because of the added dollars for the family budget. Perhaps it is still true in some cases. But agencies are gradually becoming more selective in their recruitment, and the people becoming foster parents are better motivated than before. We are likely to see a greater development of professional foster care, where the parent would be paid a significant amount, perhaps comparable to what could be earned at a full-time job, and where he or she will be required to undergo specialized training on child care and methods of treatment. This kind of foster parent will be expected to help children who may be retarded, handicapped or emotionally disturbed so that they can live in a family and community rather than in a residential institution.

When should children be placed in foster care?

The theory of foster care is quite sound. Only the practice need be changed. There are children and families who need foster care on a temporary basis in order to weather a crisis. Too often, however, the alternatives for the family are not explored or may not be available. Homemaker services and day-care services could help to prevent foster care in the first place by relieving the burden of parents in crisis without removing the child from them. Greater availability of community-based health and mental health services can solve a problem before it becomes a family crisis. And, of course, an improvement in the general welfare of society, especially the provision of adequate income and sufficient employment opportunity, could help prevent social problems from occurring.

In addition to the children who are victims of family crises, foster care can be valuable as a community-based alternative to institutionalization of various "problem" children – delinquents, the emotionally disturbed, the handicapped and the retarded. It has been successfully used in many states both in easing a child who has been in an institution back to community and family life, and in short-term treatment of a child whose behavior would, in the past, have warranted institutionalization. As the cruelty and regressiveness of institutions become more and more apparent, foster care will be more and more prevalent.

What rights do foster children have?

They are at the mercy of the child welfare agency which has legal custody and/or guardianship of them, and the court which temporarily cut off the rights of their parents. In fact, they have even fewer rights than their foster parents, who may have a contract with the agency spelling out their rights, duties and responsibilities.

At a minimum, a foster child ought to have the right to independent legal representation when the decision is being made to put him in foster care in the first place. He needs an advocate at least as much as his parents and the child welfare agency do. Once in foster care, the child has no rights when a decision is made to move him from one foster home to another or, when the time comes, to decide whether he should return to his biological family, remain in foster care, or be freed for adoption. At those key times, someone ought to speak solely for the child and make sure that the agency and the foster parents have his best interests uppermost in their minds.

ALL KINDS OF ADOPTION

11/ Transracial Adoption

THE Newells live in one of those cities that seem to have sprung up in the mid-nineteen-fifties. Pete manages a package store; Ann runs the household, is on the local school board, and is active in the cause of children's rights. They live in a single-family home, in a racially mixed neighborhood. They are the parents of five children and two part-time foster children. Two of their children were adopted across racial lines.

The Newells love children. They had biologically produced two boys and a girl, and were ready to try for a fourth, when Ann came across an article in *Good Housekeeping* magazine, telling of the plight of homeless American Indian children. She was taking her last month's supply of birth control pills, as she says "to give you an idea of how close we were to conceiving a fourth child." Pete was given the magazine at dinnertime. Ann told us: "It was more an issue of why not adopt, than why adopt. There certainly were more than enough kids who needed homes.

Why produce another one if there were already children to love?" Pete needed more time to think about it – typical of most men entering adoption – but he was willing to start an investigation into the adoption. The magazine instructed readers to write for the name of an agency in their area which would do an adoption study, and Ann did so.

Looking back now, the Newells know they entered their first adoption naïvely. Since they already had two boys and one girl, they asked for a daughter, if possible, but if not, a boy was fine too. They realized there would be some objections from a few friends, but felt that those few were not crucial to their life. Those closest to them were very enthusiastic.

Since the agency had processed only a handful of transracial adoptions prior to theirs, the social worker was almost as naïve as they were. Pete says: "Our greatest learning experience came from meeting with other parents who had adopted children of other races; that, and of course, being parents to our new daughter."

When Tracy arrived, she was not quite one year old. They knew she had been well cared for by her foster family, because of her easy ability to form warm relationships. Though somewhat confused the first few days, she quickly settled into the very busy life of being a member of the Newell family.

The Newells' own sensitivity to being a multiracial family came quickly. When they had gone through the adoption process, the worker at the agency had asked them if they would consider a mixed black-white child, one already in their home state, rather than an Indian from far away. "We felt we weren't ready to cope with a child who was black, that an Indian child would be more like ourselves, and therefore we would have less racial problems as she grew," Ann says. "We had had her less than a week when the realization came through. I was bathing her, and she was all wet and wiggly – I studied her very closely. I knew then that she was beautiful for herself, and her copper skin was an asset. Everyone should be appreciated for himself, not for a mold others would like to fit him into."

A year later, the Newells were ready for another child. The adoption experience was so right for them that they had no doubts that they would again adopt. "Actually, our biggest problem this time was convincing the worker we didn't care whether we got a boy or a girl, since we had two of each. She kept saying a decision would make it easier for her; we kept saying it didn't matter. We did know we wanted a mixed black-white child; how dark was unimportant."

The Newells' fifth child was another girl. This time the baby was a newborn infant, and Ann was crushed that they had to wait an extra week to get her because she was ill with the flu. "It seemed so unfair; even though I had never seen her, that baby was mine, and how could anyone keep us apart!"

Now the Newell family has been together for five years. They have two foster daughters, who stay with them on a part-time basis, and though they say their family is completed, neither Ann nor Pete is willing to state that the decision is irrevocable. "You can never tell what will happen," Pete says.

The family is a happy one, where each child is treasured for himself. "They have separate interests and friends, not because of their colors, but because of their natures. All the children know about adoption, and accept our family as the way a family should be. Tracy is deeply proud that she is an American Indian, and we encourage it. She loves when we serve cornbread, and never misses the chance to tell a visitor that corn is an Indian food, and they are eating an American Indian meal. We share her pride, and feel part of it ourselves. She also is proud that she came to us the way she did. She is able to appreciate the fact that she has had three families – first her biological mother, then her foster family, and now us – and all of them have wanted the best possible for her. She knows we're a real family, and will always be together."

The baby is almost four. She knows she is a different color, but hasn't made any comments based on race – yet! They aren't concerned about what will happen when she does: "Don't forget, we've done it before."

The Newells say they have experienced very little prejudice. "Sometimes in the market, a person will come up to my oldest daughter, and ask who the little black child is she's pushing in the basket. Maureen will just say, 'She's my sister,' and prance away." Both Newells are as hard on black racists as on white ones, and feel that a racist attitude does not help family life.

Ann Newell says: "It's easy to be prejudiced, and teach children how to be bigots. Hopefully our children will learn to appreciate each person for the individual values they have, be it race, religion, national origin, or some special talent. All families, even one-race families, should be this way. If one aspect of a person's life is so overwhelming that it consumes all other parts of a personality, that person is not going to be a whole individual. We know we will encounter some problems as our kids grow, but we consider them challenges, not problems, and issues that will make each member of the family a better person."

We live in a racist society. Black-white relationships have never been equal in this country. First, we sanctioned the enslavement of black people; Abraham Lincoln technically freed them, but they have never as a class achieved true equality with the dominant white majority. More than economic suppression is involved; it comes down to the fact that white people have essentially thought of themselves as better than blacks. There is much racial tension in America today, and unless we all learn to live with and appreciate one another in a meaningful way, there is little hope for racial peace.

While prejudice seems a part of life to many people, it is not always so. Transracial marriages have long taken place, and now transracial adoptions are occurring with enough frequency to focus attention on them.

A survey of over 400 adoption agencies showed that approximately 35 percent of all adoptions of black children in each of the years from 1968 through 1971 have been by white families.[1]

Transracial adoption is very controversial. It is not practiced by all agencies, and its status has fluctuated from time to time. Agencies had long wondered about what to do with their hard-to-place children. One worker from a progressive agency told us, "In the early nineteen-sixties we were beginning to cautiously place a trickle of mixed-racial children. When we saw it worked, we decided this could be an excellent opportunity of getting children and families together. When the requests started coming in for the Indian children, we also mentioned the black children we already had. We learned a valuable lesson about publicity. Agencies will find far more homes for children if they actively recruit them. Parents can't adopt children they don't know about."

Parents who adopted the racially mixed children formed small groups, as much to have social contact with other persons who had adopted similar children as for any other reasons. As their number grew, and as the agencies became aware that there was a market for the many children for whom there had formerly been no homes available, the numbers of these transracial adoptions grew. Parents, too, sometimes in conjunction with agencies, sometimes on their own, publicized the children who awaited homes. In many places now there are waiting lists for transracial and black babies, just as there are for white babies.

As the numbers of such adoptions grew, interest and curiosity about them also grew. Several books have been written with transracial adoption as the main theme. Black people began to focus attention on these adoptions. Criticisms were raised about placing black children in white homes; black homes should be found instead. Black social workers complained and criticized to the point where many agencies that placed children across racial lines have severely limited these adoptions, or have temporarily stopped them altogether. What will become of this type of adoption? And of the families who have already adopted children in this manner?

Is transracial adoption a second-best alternative? We

contend that it is not; that in itself, transracial adoption is a first choice for many families, and that it can be the best alternative for the children as well. We also acknowledge that we feel this as white people, and that it is a personal point of view, not shared by everyone. Like many blacks (not all) who feel that transracial adoption is second-best, so do many of the white adoptive families. They say that any black home would be best for such a child, but, since none was available, and they could love this child, they adopted him.

Black social workers feel that foster care in a black home, or even an institution with many black children, if no adoptive black family can be found, is preferable to adoption by a white family. They believe that a black child in a white family will not grow up sufficiently motivated to become an effective fighter for political, social and economic equality. They feel that every black person should fully participate in that struggle.

As long as transracial adoption exists, the controversy will undoubtedly continue. Certain important issues have emerged from it so far. First is the fact that there are relatively few adoptions by black families. Since most agencies are staffed by white workers, black families have thought of them as part of the white establishment, and thus not to be dealt with unless necessary. As more agencies take on black and minority workers, and as more agencies move into black neighborhoods, black adoptions will likewise increase.

Second, the economic myths about adoption have not limited themselves to white families. Black people, too, have felt that a family needs to own a home, have so much money in the bank, and so on before being able to adopt. And since more black families than white are in the lower income brackets, they have felt themselves out of the running. We hope that they will be reached by social workers and others who will tell them that economic resources no longer are a major factor in adoption. Love and the desire to parent are what counts. After all, not everyone was born into a rich family! In certain instances, black families may also be eligible for subsidy funds, already mentioned, which aid families in adopting a child.

Third, there are black children who need homes. As long as there are not enough black families available for these children, other homes must be found.

In addition to encouraging black families to adopt, agencies must put much time and effort into the transracial adoptions which have already taken place, as well as those which are being considered. When transracial adoption began, neither parents nor social workers knew quite what to expect. It is probably justified to say that everyone approached it idealistically. Now there are many workers trained in this area, and many experienced parents who are willing and capable of sharing their experiences and the lessons they have learned from them. Here is a list of some of the more relevant pointers to keep in mind, especially for the family contemplating transracial adoption.

1. A family who adopts transracially is no longer a white family. By taking in a person of another race, the family has an obligation to share the child's heritage with all the other members of the family, just as they will share their heritage with the child they have just adopted. Any attempts to "whitewash" the child or to turn him into some-

one he isn't shows an inability to deal with a biracial family. If the family is not ready to be proud of the child for what he himself is, they have no business adopting him. They must be ready to help the child participate in cultural activities relating to his heritage, as well as to stock the shelves with American Indian or black history books. They need to learn and participate themselves in events relating to the child's racial heritage. Preferably, they should live in a community where the family can have contact with many types of families. It is also nice to be friendly with families who have adopted children like theirs; the children can then see they are not the only ones with this lifestyle.

2. Although agencies will sometimes allow a family to specify the degree of darkness of the child they adopt, the family should ask themselves this question: Are we adopting a light child because we cannot cope with the blackness of a dark child? Several families we talked with said that these were their initial thoughts; only after adoption did they discover that the shade was unimportant to them. This concern with "degree of blackness" seems to be something families should work out before they adopt. If a family is comfortable only with a light child, they may really be trying to reject the fact that the child is black at all. Is this fair to the child? He may be cheated out of his cultural heritage and racial identity, and thus subject to serious problems as he grows up.

3. No matter how light a mixed black-white child may be, society will always consider him black. While a family can stand back and say, "Well, he is half white," all most people will see is the black.

4. There are certain identity needs that people can get only from those who are like themselves. It is easy to nod in agreement when we suggest that a family who adopts a child with physical disabilities let him have contact with similarly disabled adults to discuss matters that will be helpful to him as he grows. It seems harder to accept that the same holds true of white families who adopt black children. These children are going to have to go out and face a racist society. Maybe not while they are toddlers or in grade school, but sooner or later, they will have needs which only black people can serve. The adopting family should encourage contact with black or mixed racial families, and not be afraid of it – either for the children, or for anyone else in the family. A service agencies often render transracial families is group meetings with black counselors and families. Such sessions can only be a growing experience.

5. When adopting a transracial child, the parents must consider it a first-best choice. Many families approach transracial adoption with no fertility problems. They have no need to add one biologically. They have decided to adopt a child who is more in need of a home than the traditional white, healthy baby, and feel they have love to share with another child. Since it is a matter of choice, they enter into it because they want this child for himself. (We hope they do not enter it as a result of some white, liberal rescue fantasy.)

Some families, especially now, enter into transracial adoption because no white babies are available. We do not criticize this practice, but ask all concerned agencies, and parents alike, to work, think and discuss as much as possible before the adoption occurs. Being desperate to adopt a child may cloud a family's latent racist feelings, and these must be worked out – for the child's sake. Preferably, they can be worked out prior to the adoption, perhaps by talking with a couple who has adopted transracially. Agencies can usually put a family into contact with a transracial family or a parents' group in the area.

6. Black arguments against transracial adoptions have many levels. The most cogent one is the argument alluded to above that the blacks in America are a small minority, and, in order to gain rights as persons and as a race that they have been denied for so long, it is necessary for each black person to help in that cause. A black child adopted into a white family may therefore be politically lost, and a member of white society.

This feeling is something that families who have adopted across racial lines will have to deal with. It will not do for them to pass it off as simply a racist point of view, and as irrelevant as the white racist who is against transracial adoption.

They must believe that every child is entitled to a permanent home and family. The ability to love and value each child for his own worth is of utmost importance in helping the child develop his self-image as a person, and as a member of a race, as he grows up. It is a feeling a child can learn only in a family of his own, not in a foster home or an institution. Racial identity is secondary if a child does not have a sense of being needed and loved for himself. Only parents can give this to him.

If a white family adopts a black child, because of a desire to love and cherish him as he is and because he is a person and a black person, this is good. They can instill in him the personal values and feelings that are common to all people, no matter what their race. They can also tell him by their attitudes and living that his blackness is something to be proud of and to develop as he grows. And he can help them and his white brothers and sisters understand what being black means. And contact with other black persons and with other interracial families will show him he is not alone in his situation.

This kind of family can show the way to a truly integrated society which reflects the brotherhood of man.

White parents have to take a chance with the issue of racism. The Newells seem to express the feeling well when they say: "There are risks involved, but our girls might not have ever had families if we had not adopted them. Of course, we don't know what will happen when they are teen-agers. But we love them and are proud of each of them for themselves and their racial heritage and identity. And we're proud of them because they are our children. We are determined that our family will turn out well, and this determination makes it right for us. If families and people aren't willing to try, the world itself will never have a chance."

12/ The Child with Special Needs

Mary and Peter Andrews are both teachers. They had been married a little over two years when Peter started doing volunteer work at a local school for the retarded. He became very involved with this work as he discovered many of the children had not been allowed to use their intellectual capacities. He persuaded Mary to spend an afternoon a week helping also, and within a month they came across a little boy named Jimmy.

Jimmy was six and a half, and suffered from a spinal disorder which gave him no control of the lower half of his body. He had come to the school as a tiny baby, and had been there most of his life. Because he was so appealing and seemed able to learn, two aides had spent extra time with him his first three years and convinced the state to find him a foster home. One was found, but the foster mother had three small children, and lived in a second-floor apartment – wholly unsuited for a child in a wheelchair. Unable to give him much attention or care, the family returned Jimmy to the state school before his fourth birthday. He never left again, until the Andrewses came.

Peter was immediately captivated by Jimmy and felt he did not belong there. He and Mary had no children as yet and planned to wait at least another year before starting a family. Having worked with children with special needs in the past, they seriously considered adopting a child in the future. They felt that now was not the time, Peter recalls. Since Jimmy had no family to visit him, the Andrewses began taking him for afternoon and daytime visits. "We finally asked the school if we could become his foster parents 'part-time.' We weren't home on weekdays, but wanted him on weekends. His social worker arranged this, and Jimmy spent his weekends here. He learned very quickly, we discovered, and we showed him fire stations and supermarkets, things he had never seen. It took a while before we were able to persuade the school authorities to send him to a school for the physically handicapped but at last we got him transferred," Peter says.

"We missed him very much, because the other school was fifty miles away, and the weekend visits were not enough. We fell in love with him, and decided to rework our family plans around him."

Mary and Peter got together with the social worker, who agreed to let Jimmy live with them on a trial basis. Mary was able to enroll him in the neighborhood public school, and Jimmy came to live. "Our one problem has been school. His first year, his classroom was on the first floor, but after that he would have been upstairs, and the school has no elevator. The school system wanted to put him in a school on the other side of the city, so we've pulled him out, and put him in a private school near us. Since several other children on our block go there too, he has friends, but we're both angry that schools don't do more for kids with handicaps."

A year and a half after Jimmy came, Mary gave birth to a boy. The Andrewses both wanted Jimmy's new brother to be a legal one, and not a foster brother, so they seriously considered adopting Jimmy. They also became members of a group of parents whose children had physical handicaps, as well as members of an adoptive parents' group.

"Our only problem was money. Crutches, wheelchairs, doctor visits and physical therapy add up. We worked hard on a bill in our state legislature to provide monetary aid for adoptions, hoping it would enable not only us, but other families, to adopt children who require extra care," Mary says. "As soon as that bill passed, we applied for aid – and got it. It didn't take us long after that to get to court and finalize our adoption."

Man has always considered both mental and physical strength to be prime virtues. Many primitive societies used to put to death infants who were found to be crippled or otherwise infirm. Other societies, our own included, often cast these children aside and locked them away from most of its members, granting them only custodial care. In past civilizations and in remote cultures today there has been rationalization for these acts. Darwin called this "the survival of the fittest." Each person was needed to do his share of work, or else the society might not survive. In modern, developed societies, where there is enough differentiation so that each member can contribute on his or her own level, handicapped children are rejected most often because of shame or an inability on the part of parents to cope with an extraordinary child.

Certainly, in the past, such handicapped children were never considered adoptable. It did not occur to social workers, or to prospective parents, that these "different" children would be welcomed and valued in some homes. As a greater proportion of children with special needs awaited homes and fewer "normal" children became available, both parents and social workers began seriously to consider adoption for these "hard-to-place" children. In increasing numbers, children who would have spent their lives in institutions or as wards of the state are now finding permanent and loving families.

Social workers have discovered that placement of children with special needs requires more of their time and skill than placing children without special needs. Prospective parents usually take more time to decide finally that they can be a family to such a child. This means more sessions with the social worker and, in the case of older children, more shared experiences with the child before placement.

Many thousands of the children who now await homes and families have physical and mental disabilities of varying severity. Usually they are referred to as "handicapped" children. But just as there is no such thing as an adopted child, only a child who becomes part of a family through the legal process of adoption, so is there no such thing as a handicapped child, only a child who happens to have a specific disability. These disabilities range from mild short-term disorders to serious life-threatening illnesses. The child of special needs may be blind, deaf or missing a limb; he may be a child with a correctable or permanent heart defect; he may have orthopedic problems or a congenital deformity. Children with cerebral palsy, epilepsy, neurological conditions and mental retardation are in need of parents. Children with various learning disabilities with normal intelligence, as well as those who have emotional problems, need families who will love, understand and accept them.

A family considering adoption of a child with special needs must first investigate their motives. A desire to aid a child in trouble is not enough, for adoption implies mutual love. The couple must be willing to be responsible parents to a child, and not a nursemaid to the sick. The desperation a family feels when healthy children are not available is itself not a sufficient motive. Such impulsive adoptions do not necessarily develop into the love and trust essential for healthy family growth.

What is required is a unique type of family. Parents of special-needs children must have extra patience and love for children who need vast amounts of time and care. These families must be able to accept the mental and physical limitations of their child and, at the same time, help him to reach his greatest potential as he grows and matures.

Prospective parents must consider the future degree of independence the child will be able to attain. Some will always need shelter provided; others, particularly those with mental disabilities, will always be dependent to some degree on other persons for many of their needs. What burdens will this cause on a family? One method of learning about future dependence, as well as hearing firsthand about how families raise a child with a particular handicap, is to visit parents whose children have a similar disability. Discussions with adults who are similarly disabled are also helpful, since they speak from experience about what children can expect from or contribute to society.

There is no substitute for a proper medical evaluation. Social workers can show a child's picture, and describe his problems in terms of his disability or deprivation. They can offer reassuring judgments about the child's likely response to a loving and personalized environment. But social workers are not qualified to give thorough medical diagnoses or prognoses; nor can they fully and adequately describe complicated medical and emotional problems. Prospective parents should always insist on meeting the child's physician, whether he's a pediatrician or a psychiatrist, and talking personally with him. The family's own physician should examine and evaluate the child if possible. If not, he or she should speak with the agency's physician, psychiatrist or psychologist, preferably in conference with both parents and the social worker who may be following the case. If the child was in foster care, the foster parents should also be involved.

Many available children have multiple handicaps. There have been instances when a child was placed with a family who were not aware of the total health problem. We would prefer to think that the social worker who placed the child was not aware that the problems existed, either; however, some workers, for whatever reasons, neglect to interpret fully or to share pertinent medical data. As an example, one family we know adopted a child who was diagnosed as having a "learning handicap." The social worker felt that in a warm family environment the child would possibly overcome this problem. The family took the child home and soon discovered that she had a correctable vision problem, not a learning disability. Although this case ended well, it still serves to indicate that parents interested in a child should find out in advance all the physical and medical information available. Psychological testing is important, especially in an older child. Prospective parents should be sure to investigate all aspects of the child's health prior to an adoptive placement in order that they may know what they must give to the child and what the child will be able to give to them.

Medical problems often cost a lot of money. When considering adoption of the child with special needs, a family has to evaluate their financial limitations and expectations. Medical and related expenses over a number of years should be predicted as accurately as possible. Parents ought to discover whether and to what extent financial subsidies for adoption are available and whether they extend to support as well as to medical or therapeutic expenses. Agencies have this information and will tell the parents how to apply for the subsidy. In the past, many foster parents took in children with special problems, grew to love them, and wished to adopt them. However, the cost of illness and treatment was financially staggering to the family budget. Since state-sponsored programs paid for the medical care of these children only as long as they were in foster care, they would often remain unadopted, though not unwanted. Subsidy laws and programs have enabled families, foster or otherwise, to give children the extra security of legally being permanent family members by providing medical care and, at times, child support at little or no cost to the family. Where subsidy programs do not presently exist, prospective parents and other people concerned about children who languish in foster care ought to coalesce their forces and organize to bring political pressure for change. A well-planned, inclusive subsidy program based on need, such as the one in Massachusetts, not only financially aids the family and child, but has the potential to save the taxpayer money when compared with the cost of total state care.

If a family finds that financially and emotionally they are ready to provide a home for a child with special needs, there are still other matters which bear thought.

First, any other children in the family must be consulted and told of the decision. They, too, need to know as much as possible about the child's condition and prognosis. They should be aware of the amount of time his daily care will require, especially in the beginning, when routines are being established. Often this time would normally have been spent with them. Other relatives should be told of the new arrival, and parents should anticipate many questions, especially from the soon-to-be grandparents. They are often most concerned that their children will have taken on an unnecessary burden. They have to come to understand the motives of the parents and the value of the child. Most likely they will, and the child will be loved and accepted by them.

The family should investigate schooling possibilities. In some areas there are special schools and facilities available for children with various kinds of disabilities. Parents should determine whether the child could benefit from such a school, taking into account transportation arrangements and other associated costs. In certain instances, the local school system will absorb the cost of educating a child with special needs if appropriate or adequate education cannot be provided in the public system. A telephone call to the school board or to a parent in the area with a child with similar needs might provide answers to special education questions.

If the child will be going to a public school, the parents may want to visit in advance, meet the teachers and see the physical layout. A child in a wheelchair, as we have pointed out, whose classroom is on the second floor needs an elevator available or special individual arrangements. If appropriate facilities and plans cannot be made at the local school, it may be necessary to consider a school in a different area. However, if the child has friends in the neighborhood, he may not want to go to a school far from home.

The physical layout of the family home may be crucial to certain children. A two-story or colonial home is more limiting than a ground-floor apartment or ranch house to a child in a wheelchair. Can the house be renovated with ramps for easier access? Changing light switches or the location and height of various fixtures, and improvising a lightbulb connection to the doorbell so a deaf child may "see" the bell ring are changes which will make the child at ease and more independent in his daily life. A hyperactive child will do better in fairly barren rooms than in cluttered or crowded ones.

The neighborhood and peers are important. Although the child may be physically, mentally or emotionally disabled, social growth and development is as important for him as any other child. While adults are able (usually) to curb the instinct to stare or ask questions about a child who is visibly different, youngsters (usually) cannot. Parents should be able to field questions in a manner which is helpful to the inquiring youngster and, at the same time, gives a positive image to their child. For example, to a question like: "How come Johnny has funny things on his legs?" a response may be: "Those are braces. When Johnny was a baby, he had a disease called polio which made his legs very weak. They were so weak that he couldn't stand on them. The doctors made these special braces for him and they help him to get around. He might not be able to run, but he can play chess, go to the movies, and be a Cub Scout."

Some neighborhoods are warm and understanding. Adults and children are open and accepting, and the new child will be appreciated for the values he has, not the skills he lacks. In other places, neighbors will be shy and unsure. Here the adoptive family must make the first overtures and invite children to visit and play in the home. Sometimes only a few visits are needed; at other times many are required before the new child is accepted into the neighborhood social circle. Peer play teaches not only socialization, but specific skills as well.

Unfortunately, there are times, particularly with mental or emotional disability, where the child may not be accepted by the neighbors. This doesn't mean that the child must always be alone, but the parent must carefully structure and plan all playtimes. Often by providing interesting games and toys indoors as well as playground equipment outside, they can attract youngsters to the yard who may otherwise be reluctant to come. Sometimes, one can plan visits with other children, perhaps those who are similarly handicapped. Other times, the family may be the sole source of socialization outside of school. How can parents help a child to deal with the possible rejection of the neighborhood? Other parents who have undergone this problem and psychiatrists, psychologists and social workers can be of valuable help in adjusting to rejection.

Children with special needs require great time and energy on a day-to-day basis. Parents must be certain to learn as much as possible about the talents that will be required of them after adoption. They may have to learn how to control an epileptic seizure, give physical therapy, or read a Braille alphabet. The more they know, the better parents they will be to the child. Physicians, visiting nurses and occupational or physical therapists will prove invaluable resources to the entire family.

As the new family gets established and routines and patterns for daily life are set, the parents must be willing to turn their attention to themselves. They will need time for relaxation, and shouldn't have to be "tied down" to the new child. Friends, neighbors and relatives may be able to learn to care for the child on a short-term basis, just so mom can have a day out shopping, or both parents can enjoy a movie or the theater. Many families are able to find persons they trust to care for their children for an extended time so that they may have a much-needed vacation. Parents of similarly handicapped children may be willing to "trade" by taking turns baby-sitting for each other's children. Sometimes parents do not know someone who can help out and will have to resort to professional aid in order to have personal freedom. Time away from home doesn't mean they aren't good parents to these children, but rather that they have the normal human needs for rest and relaxation. We don't know of a single parent who didn't appreciate their child (disabled or not) more after a vacation!

Of all the elements that need thought before adopting a child with special needs, the child himself is the prime concern. First and foremost, he is a person with the capacity to love and be loved, even though in certain cases of emotional or mental illness, these capacities do not come within the bounds most people have come to accept. His handicap may make aspects of life more difficult for him and for those around him as well. But it does not affect his humanness. As a human being, he has a right to a home and family. It is unfortunate that not everyone can return the love of such a child, or even accept it from him. Many people can, however, and often they are not aware of this ability until such a child enters their lives. There are numbers of people who had no intention of adopting a child with special needs, but, through foster care or work in a state institution, came to know and love a particular child and want him for their own.

No one should ever persuade another person to adopt this kind of child. The desire to love and nurture him must grow and develop naturally. But neither should anyone discourage another person from considering an adoption of this sort. Social workers, physicians or other interested parties who say, "These things never work out," "The problems aren't worth it," or "He's better off in an institution," ought to deal with their own personal feelings about these children before discouraging others.

The satisfactions of raising these children may not always be the traditional ones we have come to accept. But perhaps it is time to consider how relevant our values are. We should be able to appreciate each person on his own terms.

In addition to loving a special child for himself, parents must also be able to instill in him a sense of identity and self-worth. The child's independence, rather than dependence, should be the goal. Visits to similarly handicapped adults can be very valuable to the growing child as well as his parents. While his parents may be able to help him with day-to-day living problems, there are some questions that can be answered only by another person who has undergone the same experiences. Those aspects of his life which we all have in common – the ability to love, feel and learn – should be stressed, and those which make him different should be looked upon as characteristics which make him, like each of us, a unique human being.

Society's past neglect of children with special needs has resulted in today's tragedy of thousands of children in foster care and institutions who have been denied their right to a permanent family and to development to their fullest potential. The task at hand is for public and private agencies, professionals and parents to rescue these children by making possible their adoption by families who can provide love and understanding. With the decrease in availability of infants, the future of adoption will, in great measure, depend on the success of this effort.

13/ Older Children

CHRISTINE was fourteen years old when she went to stay with the Browns. It was the twelfth foster family she had lived in and the second in three months. Prior to that, she had spent three years in a group home run by a child welfare agency. She had been verbally and physically abusive to others, and the institution considered her one of their failures. She came to the Browns because most of her other foster families couldn't "handle" her.

John and Carol Brown have three biological children; John sells real estate, Carol is a housewife. Shortly after the birth of their third child, they were at a cocktail party and entered into a conversation on foster children. A priest was talking of the need for families for youngsters who were placed in "reform" schools because they created problems in school or had run away from home. Many came from bad family situations, and the atmosphere at the detention centers was detrimental to them. Carol Brown says, "We told him we would be interested in trying to help such a child – we had two extra beds – and I think we had our first foster child a week later. It happened so fast we really didn't have time to think about how it would affect our lives."

Christine was their fourth foster child. Although both her parents are alive, Christine has not seen or heard from them for several years. She was two when the court removed her and her eight brothers and sisters from the home because of the incapacity of her parents, attributed to alcoholism. She has lost touch with all but one sister. After two and a half years with the Browns, Christine approached them to ask if they would adopt her. "We said yes, without question, although we had never considered it. We thought because her parents were alive, we couldn't legally adopt her. But we asked the agency and they said we wouldn't have any problems since there had been no effort by the parents to sustain the relationship. After that, we discussed finances with Christine. As long as she stayed a foster child, the state would pay for her college, clothing, and even her allowance. As a member of a four-children family, we couldn't guarantee her some of those extras. We told her our love didn't depend on the adoption. She still wanted us to adopt her, so we applied for subsidy aid, which we were able to get. Now she has the security of being a legal Brown, and the financial aid of the state until her twenty-first birthday."

The Browns had a sense of commitment to Christine right from the beginning. When she was suspended from school for hitting a teacher, they were at school the next morning to plead Christine's case. They explained to the principal about her troubled past, and how rejection would only increase her problems. The school agreed to take her back and work with her. "Although she now attends another school, she still corresponds with some of her former teachers there," Carol says proudly.

There were difficulties at home, too. Christine would be rude, or not willing to share in the housework or clean her room. But by being patient, and making it known she was "just like everyone else" in the family, the family helped Christine slowly but surely become just that.

"There were many times I went to bed thinking we couldn't make it through another day, but we did. We didn't do anything special that I can think of, but we did allow ourselves to bend a little. You have to be flexible, or else it won't work. If I had to give advice to someone that would be it. You have to be flexible. They're already people, and you can't change or diminish their pasts. You have to be willing to take them as they are, and then all become a family."

Christine is seventeen now. How does she feel about her adoption or her past? "Nothing is different with us as a family, but we know the security is important to her.

"She'll sometimes come to me and say she hates her ex-mother and -family, but we always tell her it's not good to hate. I know she's written her ex-mother since she's been here, but she's never received a reply. Maybe when she's married, she'll look her up, but what's most important to her now is that everywhere she goes, she's Christine Brown."

The Browns probably don't think of themselves as an extraordinary family, but they are. They have the patience, love and flexibility to take an older child into their home and let her be one of their own. No matter how simple they may make it seem, adoption of the older child is both challenging and difficult.

The Browns adopted their foster child, which is one common way for a family to come together with an older child. Some agencies frown on foster parents adopting their foster children, primarily because the biological parents may know the foster parents from previous visits. We believe that this limitation has been carried much too far — often in the form of a complete prohibition against such adoptions. In the case of older children who have lived with foster parents for quite a while and in cases where there was no contact with the biological parents, such a rule hurts only the child.

Some older children are adopted by relatives, and there is usually a solid relationship in existence prior to the time the family considers adoption. Most states have assumed that such a relationship exists and exempt relative adoption from the general requirement of agency investigations. We question that exemption, especially where "relative" is defined broadly to include distant relatives. The welfare of the child might well suffer just as much in a relative adoption as any other; an agency investigation, even in an independent adoption, would add a bit of protection for the child.

Since more and more families are becoming interested and actually adopting older children, some agencies have begun to concentrate their efforts on finding homes for them. From talking with adoption workers, and from listening to the experiences of many families, we have seen certain characteristics of older child adoptions emerge.

Most important is the ability to be flexible. When a

family enters into the adoption of an older child, they are taking a child who already has opinions, feelings and a code of values. In a way it is more like a marriage than becoming a parent, because there must be a longer period of adjustment to one another, and parent and child alike have both positive and negative feelings. In many instances a child will voluntarily leave the adoptive family because he feels he cannot fit in its structure. The parent should not look for a child to change over and make into a reflection of his own personality. Rather, he should understand that a child has thoughts and feelings he must be willing to listen to and respect, just as the child will listen to and learn to respect the parent's. Much of what he will be in the future may already have been formed by past experiences. A family has to be willing to accept this, and on occasion modify their points of view and feelings to encompass those of the child. They cannot erase the five, ten or even fifteen years which have preceded their relationship, and must be willing to adapt parts of it into their lifestyle.

As the child responds or reacts to the new home, the family must change with him. The expectations for the other children in the family cannot always be imposed on a newcomer who doesn't understand what family life is about. Nor can he be expected to possess the same talents as other members of the family. He will already be an individual. He might be interested in baseball, but he might lack certain skills the other children have, despite the interest. If the skills are too important to the rest of the family, this child will automatically sense rejection. If on the other hand he is appreciated for the joy he shares in the game, and the skills he possesses in other areas, say artistic talents, are appreciated and built upon, the family has a much better chance of making a go of the adoption. The children, as well as the parents, will have to put forth maximum effort.

The parents should be flexible not only in what they may expect from a child, but also in how they react to him. Older adopted children will make their parents angry, often angrier than they have ever been. The child may misbehave, be rude or destructive, time and time again. Because there is often no rationality to the child's acts, the parents cannot just sit down and say, "You shouldn't take cookies from the cookie jar before dinner because it will spoil your dinner," or "I don't like it when you take those cookies. You're not considerate of me," on the seventh consecutive day when the child has robbed the cookie jar. Rather, the parent has to show he is angry: "Go to your room for taking those cookies!" They can talk together later about why it's wrong to take cookies, but what the children need is someone to react to them on an emotional level, not an intellectual one. It may be a novel idea to some families, but often direct punishment, even a whack on the bottom now and then, is the best way of saying "I care about you."

The family must also be patient. The child will be testing the parents constantly as his way of establishing whether or not the family really wants him. The more rejections the child has had in the past, the harder the adjustment will be. It takes a long time for a child who has learned that failure is part of his life to learn how to deal with acceptance and love. There is a famous children's poem which says, "Children live what they learn." Only by patience on the part of his parents will the child learn to live with love.

We were talking with a couple recently who said they would advise very strongly against adopting an older child. Two years previously, they had begun the process of adopting a five-year-old boy. The agency told the family he was bright and friendly, and the couple agreed that he was. But they found him "unresponsive"; he did not react to the love they shared with him. The agency took the child back after four months. Instead of success, both the adoption and the child met with failure – a failure he will remember.

We cannot say whether or not this placement should have occurred. The couple certainly did not appear to have had the patience or the commitment to see the adoption through. But this story leads us nicely to the next important factor of older child placements: the relationship between the agency and the adoptive family.

Adoption agencies and parents have to work very closely together in order for the adoption to succeed. The more they know about one another, the better the chances for an appropriate placement. Perhaps this family lacked the encouragement of a social worker, or the knowledge that these adoptions of older children are long, hard work. Often only the caseworkers can share that type of information with a parent. If you're interested in adopting an older child, it is important to have a social worker who has had experience with such a child. The more she/he knows about your particular child, the better able she/he will be to help you as a family decide whether the adoption or the child is right for your family.

Because the child has a developed personality, the agency will be extremely interested in all aspects of your family's life, and will want to know about any other children already in the family. Optimally, they will explain to you about foster care, child abuse, and the emotional problems an older child will have adjusting to a new family, no matter how stable that family already is. It would do well for the agency to have two or three particular children in mind when studying a family. This way the families can learn about the particular adjustment problems they will be facing, and the agency can decide if one family will be better for a certain child than another family might be. A family with three daughters which goes into adoption looking for the son they never had might find that their home is better equipped for raising and loving a certain girl who is in need of a home at that time. They may have advantages and talents that would help this girl and they may discover that the boy who attracted their attention needs a family with brothers, not sisters. A family with two small children that wants to adopt a ten-year-old may discover that the one they had in mind is emotionally not prepared to deal with young siblings, but requires a family where he won't have competition from younger children. The child's needs are every bit as important as those of the adoptive family.

The relationship with the social worker can be as important to the child as to the parent, but not always in a positive way. To many a child, the social worker has often come to be a constant companion. He or she is the person who takes him from family to family, and talks with the child about his changing life. For many children, the social worker is someone to rely on, someone to trust. And for these children, the friendship can be kept up long after the adoption has been finalized.

For other children, the social worker can be a threat to their new home life. Each time the worker comes to visit, the child fears the adoption is over. "He's come to take me back again." The family has to be sensitive to the reactions of each particular child.

The same is true of contact with previous foster parents and friends from the old neighborhood. Some children will be able to visit their past life, and then come home to the new one. For others the emotional tug is too strong, and they may feel less sure of where they belong after a visit. For them, it is better to let old friends come see them in their new home. Or maybe to consider discontinuing these relationships. Once again, the parents have to be sensitive to the needs of the child as an individual.

Where do these older children come from? Some of them are children who were given up for adoption at birth. Because they were mixed-racial or black, because they had a physical problem, or simply because there was no family for them at the time, they were placed in foster care or institutions, where they have lived ever since. Some were given love and good-quality care; others, especially those in institutions, were given the bare minimum for existence. Other children were removed from their biological families by the courts. Perhaps they had been abused or mistreated; some had been deserted. Many are children who had been placed in foster care by their mothers. Illness, desertion or lack of money often caused the separation; eventually they were released for adoption. Some are children whose parents have died, and there was no relative willing or able to care for them. All wait for and need families.

Not all of these children are young. Some have already

entered their teen-age years, and have intense understanding of their situations. Even though they may have never existed in a family setting, they want the opportunity to try. Some have had adoptive placements previously which for one reason or another did not work out. Many have been in long-term foster care, and have had to leave the families after developing deep emotional bonds. Others leave foster care scarred by their bad experiences.

How long does the adoption of an older child take? After a family and a child have been selected for one another, a transition process takes place. The new parents have already seen a picture of the child when they meet with him for the first time. If he is old enough, he is also aware that the family is interested in adopting him, and knows that he also has the privilege of saying no if it doesn't work out. The older the child, the longer the time between initial meeting and placement. For a preschooler there may be several daytime visits, and perhaps an overnight trip before placement. The more cautious the agency, the longer the transition, although some parents report that a period of several weeks seems to be too long for a small child. The going back-and-forth is more trying on some children than one big move would be.

Bigger children need the time. On first visits, everyone is on good behavior, and probably tense as well. As more day and overnight and weekend visits occur, the child and family will fall into more familiar behavior patterns. The honeymoon will end. Beautiful manners will degenerate, and calm parents will find difficult behavior they might not have expected in the beginning.

Will there be emotional problems? There are bound to

be some, once again depending on the age of the child and the number of moves he's made in his lifetime.

How and when problems surface vary from child to child. Some may react hostilely in the neighborhood or in school, as did Christine Brown. Others can react hostilely to parents or other new siblings. One mother we know spent many nights worrying about whether she was harming her relationship with her two existing children as the child she adopted spent night after night waking the other children and destroying their toys. "We wouldn't have been able to make it if the other kids hadn't been able to understand and cooperate. It's really hard for them. What made the difference was they knew that Martha might never have a family if we didn't adopt her. They were old enough (ten and eight) to want to help us try."

This family eventually had psychiatric help with their new daughter, but that was two years ago, and today there's barely a trace of past problems. As do the Browns, they emphasize the importance of being flexible when you adopt an older child. "A family really can't conceive of what happens when they adopt an older child. Your whole life seems to spin, but if you can make it work, it's fantastic."

Another family has other advice. "You have to be tough. These are children who have been raised with all kinds of inconsistencies, and they don't know who they are or where they belong. You can't say to them, 'You shouldn't do this' and 'You shouldn't do that.' Being judgmental tears them apart more. You have to say, 'That's wrong to do,' not 'That's wrong for *you* to do.' Letting them know there's a right and a wrong, and showing them your genuine anger lets them know you care. People are very anxious to protect these kids, but you can't, or they just may not adjust. You have to act from the gut sometimes, not from the brain."

We asked a social worker to single out what were to her the most important qualities for parents who adopt older children. Her reply: "The parents have to be secure in themselves, and secure with one another. Their relationship has to be steady and strong, one where they can communicate openly and honestly about the good and the bad. This kind of couple has the strength to be supportive with each other and with the older child.

"The other quality I look for is commitment. In order to have the adoption succeed, the parents have to want to make it work. If they waver, so does the adoption. To be truthful, not all families possess these qualities, and the caseworker has to really help those other families, and decide whether they should adopt an older child at all."

Do you want to adopt an older child? Here is a checklist of things to keep in mind as you discuss it with your family.

1. Are you willing to work hard and consistently at making the adoption work? You really need to be committed.

2. Are you open-minded about your age or sex requirements? If you had wanted a six-year-old, but the agency has an eight-year-old who needs a home, could you accept that change?

3. Are you willing to be flexible in what you expect from this child? He'll already have a lifestyle and his own

thoughts. The older he is, the more firmly entrenched his own lifestyle will be.

4. Are your children going to be threatened by the adoption? Will they be willing and able to share toys, clothes and bedrooms, as well as their parents? No matter how much you may want to adopt a child, you have to consider their needs. Would next year be better for them?

5. Will you be able to discuss the adoption with your existing children, and share the excitement and end results with them?

6. Are you prepared for emotional problems the new child will have?

If you're in the process of adopting an older child now, here are a few other items to keep in mind.

1. It happens that some children who are placed in families turn out to have problems or disabilities other than those the parents know about. Always have your own doctor check the child, and be aware that unexpected problems may crop up.

2. If your child is having trouble, be willing to contact the social worker or some other professional person to help you out.

3. The older the child, the more he knows about what's happening. Finalizing the adoption will be important to him, but sometimes agencies are so busy that promised court dates might slip by. If such a delay concerns you, see if you can have a private lawyer finalize the adoption.

4. For some families who are good families and try hard, the adoption just doesn't work out. Sometimes the child's

problems are greater than the agency and parents expect; sometimes the parents and child just don't fit together.

The child's best interests are of prime importance. And it's possible that adoption might not be the best plan for him.

Adoption should be an opportunity available for all children whose parents are unable, unwilling or unfit to provide loving and responsible parental care. Too often in the past older children were forgotten, not only by their parents, but by society and its agents, the child welfare agencies. They were condemned to an insecure, unstable and changing childhood in foster care. They have a right to a better life – and the success of the Browns and many families like them indicate that their rights are gradually being fulfilled.

14/ Single-Parent Adoption

MAUREEN McCARTHY is a dental hygienist in her early forties. She is single, and the mother of two children she has adopted.

When Maureen turned thirty-five, she felt her prospects for marriage at that age were quite slim, but she wanted a family. A magazine article about single adoptive parents started her thinking for herself about adoption. She debated for well over a year before mentioning it to her family. "I felt if anything should happen to me, I would want my brothers or sister to be willing to care for my child."

Her brothers and sister were surprised but supportive, as were most of her friends, and she put in an application with a local agency.

"I was very insecure about the home study my first time; most parents are. The agency had placed three children with single parents prior to my adoption, and I was interviewed by the woman who had carried out their adoptions."

Her home study was similar to most studies, but did have some special aspects. First, the social worker wanted to be sure she had considered plans for the child in the event something incapacitated her, which of course she had. Second, they were interested in her work arrangements, and the type of help she would have with her child.

Maureen decided to move from her small in-town apartment to a more residential area. She bought a small house there, and was extremely fortunate in finding a live-in housekeeper.

The agency had told her in advance that they would place only a girl with a one-parent family, and that she would be of mixed race. Maureen would have preferred a white child when she began the study, she says, "just because I never thought about it. But when they said that my child would be mixed-racial, it didn't matter. What was important was to be a family. Now I couldn't picture having any other children than my two."

Her baby was eight months old when she arrived, and Maureen took the summer off to get acquainted. She laughs when she says that she spent half her time on the telephone asking friends if the baby should be eating now, or sleeping – just like any new mother. She also says she caused much neighborhood conversation, as she and Melissa took their first few strolls. She did not enjoy the role of neighborhood curiosity piece, but came to be tolerant of the questions and stares – they finally subsided.

Maureen McCarthy is a loving mother, and within a year, she decided she wanted another child. "This time I had more trouble. Children were harder to get, and the agency had almost stopped taking applications for two-parent families. I really had to badger them long and hard."

But it was worth it. Three years later, Maureen became the mother of a son, Jamie. Although the agency did not place boys with single parents, this particular child happened to need a home, and the agency felt that Maureen would be able to provide a family for him.

"My relatives live in the country, and we spend a lot of time there. I have two married brothers, a married sister, and plenty of cousins for my children. Although they have no father, they have lots of masculine influence in their lives."

Will she ever marry? She doubts it, but has a distinct twinkle in her eyes as she says she will never eliminate the possibility.

Do her children suffer because they have no father? Jamie is only two, but Melissa is almost six and already in kindergarten. When she was in nursery school, there was to be a Fathers' Night. Maureen thought Melissa would feel left out, but the school canceled the event. "Not because of me, but because two divorced mothers put up quite a fuss. One-parent families are not peculiar to the adoption experience. I remember my social worker said, 'We accept one-parent families, but prefer a two-parent home.' I heartily agree and told her so. If you think about it, two parents are better than one, and three would probably be better than two!"

One of the most cherished reasons for adoption is the belief that each child is entitled to two parents, a father and a mother. It therefore comes as a surprise to many people that there have been at least a limited number of one-parent adoptions.

The single-parent family is not unique to adoption. There are, after all, numbers of one-parent families caused by death of one spouse, divorce, or lengthy separation, either voluntary or involuntary. Many foster homes have only one adult. But it is quite another matter to *choose* a one-parent family for a child. Although all social workers, and most single adoptive parents, agree that a two-parent home is the first choice for any child, there are numbers of hard-to-place children who are not being considered by two-parent families. Single-parent adoption has arisen to meet the needs of these children.

Such adoptions are infrequent and statistics hard to come by. Of the approximately eight thousand children placed by the Los Angeles Department of Adoptions in 1966 and 1967, forty were with single parents, only one of these with a man. The youngest adoptive parent was thirty, the oldest fifty-four. Only two of the children were returned to the agency. The children were placed in response to publicity about the hard-to-place child. Over half of the women, and the lone father, were black. As more two-parent families become interested in these children, who are black, mixed-racial and Mexican-American, there are fewer one-parent adoptions by this same agency.[1]

The single person interested in adopting a child has a nearly insurmountable task today; to find an agency, convince the agency she (he) will be a good parent, and then be able to receive a child. We have picked up many suggestions from single parents (and others) and share them here.

1. Financial insecurity is the biggest worry. Virtually all single parents must work to support themselves and their families. The salary which was adequate for one person is not going to go as far for two or even three, especially after the baby-sitter is paid. Some single parents live with their parents or other relatives, which is of great economic help in many areas, but most must fend for themselves. We noticed that most of the single parents we've met were in well-paid positions and were often highly educated. This doesn't mean education is a criterion for parenthood, just that the higher salary which is commensurate with skilled positions makes it easier for a single person to adopt.

2. Most single parents are over the age of thirty. We only know of one parent under thirty; most are closer to or well into their forties. Since these people are voluntarily taking on the tasks of both mothering and fathering, they need a lot of emotional maturity. One mother we spoke with said: "I'm approached by women in their mid-twenties who view what I do idealistically, and I always tell them idealism won't make a good parent. I don't want to appear critical of a young woman who wants to adopt, but it's difficult to be emotionally and financially secure at twenty-six."

3. The extended family is important to a one-parent family. Tied in with this is the importance of the masculine influence on children. While they will have only a mother, there is no reason why these children should be denied the companionship and advice of men. Although this is not a criterion for adoption, many agencies look for homes which will provide lots of contact with relatives or long-term male friends. Although most of the children placed are

girls, they as well as boys benefit from having grandfathers and uncles and are well aware of the loss of a father figure. One adoptive single mother, herself a psychologist, stressed the need of little girls from four to eight for a father figure, which she had seen demonstrated over and over again. She felt it was important for mothers to be able to provide some male influences, especially in these years. She also criticizes such school- or church-sponsored customs as "Fathers' Night" or "Mothers' Night," since many children have only one parent. Wouldn't a Parents' Night be a better choice?

4. A single person thinking about adoption might overlook her environment in her initial decision, but it may someday catch up to her. We know of one woman who spent her first month of motherhood in a one-room apartment. It's humorous now, but it wasn't then. Older children especially benefit from a residential neighborhood, near to school and friends. Not only the lifestyle, but the homestyle of a single parent has to be adapted to the newly formed family.

5. The social worker is bound to ask a single parent her (or his) feelings about marriage. While some single parents have been married in the past, a great many have not. Most, for one reason or another – usually age is a factor – have decided marriage is unlikely. I've never heard one mother rule it out as a possibility. Most willingly admit that children are likely to diminish the possibility rather than increase it, although some single parents do marry after adoption. In some cases, where there is an ongoing relationship with a man, the social worker has met him.

6. The baby-sitter is crucial to a one-parent family,

whether this person is a relative or someone hired to care for children. Whether for work or social life, it helps to have someone you trust care for your children. It is also helpful if the baby-sitters can be people with whom the children can develop a relationship, rather than a stream of people. It is very hard to share children with an outside person, when children develop emotional attachments to these people. But if his or her relationship to his or her parent is a good one, no child's love will be removed by a baby-sitter.

7. If possible, single-parent families should have contact with other similar families. The children then have peers with whom they can identify.

Social workers have many problems with the one-parent adoption, over and above denying a child two parents. When two-parent families were not seriously interested in hard-to-place children, it was easier for social workers to justify the one-parent home. As there are more families for these children, the prospects for adoption grow dim for single persons. Many who were denied children by an agency have searched independently in other states to find children. Some have succeeded.

Agencies are also concerned with the sexual identification of a single parent. Many social workers feel a sexual hang-up is involved, especially when a man wants to adopt. We have overheard one social worker foolishly proclaim, "What normal single man would want children?" Social workers want to be assured that women are not adopting children because of a fear of marriage, or fear of establishing a relationship with a member of the opposite sex. Although this is a private matter, it is important for the single parent to be able to instill an appreciation of both men and women in the child, so that the child can open-mindedly face the world.

Financial resources, environment, and ability to assume the functions of a parent are areas the social worker will discuss with a single parent. Also, workers are concerned that the parent have enough maturity to be able to cope with all the extra questions her/his child will have, questions such as "Why don't I have a daddy?"

Social workers have one other major problem with single-parent adoption, and it is one that deserves some thought. When an unwed mother releases a child for adoption, one of her satisfactions is that her child will be given two parents, something she cannot provide. Many agencies call her when a family has been found for her child, and it is common practice to tell her a little about the adoptive family. How can the agency explain the single-parent adoption to this girl? Will it produce guilt in her, or anger, or hostility? Should an agency not tell the biological mother her child is in a one-parent home? Or would it be simpler not to place children at all with single parents? There is no easy answer.

Single-parent adoption does have a place in society, as long as there are children who need homes. There will be obstacles all along the way, as a child realizes he has only one parent, and he is of a different color, or if he is an older or special-needs child. But we also cannot help but think how much harder life would be if these children were denied the love of even one parent.

Single parents are often asked if they feel different or strange. Often they notice that relatives and friends alike feel it is necessary to "explain" them to new persons. More and more of them are using "Ms." before their names, as it is hard for "Miss" Jones to take her children to the pediatrician's. The fewer heads that turn, the better for both them and their families.

The main difference between a single mother and a married mother – as between any two people – is one of personality. Marital status is not crucial at all. One woman put it well when she said, "I feel more like other people now that I have a family. I have more in common with my friends and relatives, and I enjoy being a woman more. I'm no better or worse than other mothers because I'm single – I'm just me."

15/ International Adoption

CAROL THORP is a social worker for a large state welfare agency. She works to make the public aware of the children who need homes. She also tries to find children who are awaiting adoption and get them together with families who want them. Carol is energetic and dedicated.

Well over a year ago, she signed her name to a list of persons, mainly social workers, who wanted to be "escorts" on a flight from Korea, bringing children to their new homes in the United States. Twice in the fall of 1972, she received telephone calls to prepare to leave, and twice her flights were canceled because of airline strikes. Finally, in December, 1972, Carol left for Korea.

Henry and Julia Jefferson have friends who adopted a Korean child. The Jeffersons, who have a young son and daughter, believe firmly in ZPG (Zero Population Growth). Ever since they had their two allotted biological children, they have thought of their family as complete – until their neighbors adopted a child. "Once we fell in love with their daughter, Sarah, we thought about it for ourselves. Although Sarah's personality initially made us think about adopting, we did it because we really love kids."

The Jeffersons contacted a local adoption agency, which did their home study. The agency does not deal directly with Korean children or any other overseas children, but works with an international adoption agency based in New York. "It was a year and a half altogether before we got the phone call saying our daughter would be coming sometime the week before Christmas. We had a picture of her which we put on the mantel, and we borrowed a book which had Korean words so that we could communicate with her. Waiting those last few weeks was awful."

Carol Thorp was much more affected by what she saw in Korea than she had believed possible. "There are five thousand babies abandoned in Korea every year. We went to one hospital, the Seoul Children's Hospital, that was only for mixed American-Korean boys aged seven to eighteen. Two of the adults who lived there were American-born and had taught many of the boys to speak English. They kept asking me to take them with me to America.

"It's quite pathetic, especially when you see these older mixed-racial children. They have no chance in their culture as it is today. They'll forever be outsiders unless they come to America, and they know it." Carol has been back less than a month and already she's working to find homes for the children she met. "While they're in the group home, at least they have each other, but who knows what will happen when they're a little older and have to leave."

Carol spent her days in Korea visiting not only the twelve children she and another social worker were bringing back with them, but also Korean social welfare agencies.

Many Americans still think that the Korean orphans are largely fathered by American servicemen as they were in the 1950's. While that may be true in Vietnam now, Korean adoptions have changed. Says Carol: "Almost all the children now are full-Korean. They're given up by the parents because of the terrible poverty. Families think the children will be better off in an orphanage than with them. They'll either leave a child on someone's doorstep, or abandon it on the streets. Eventually, the child will end up at the hospital, or more likely at a police station first. Because so many kids are abandoned, the police don't always consider getting them to a hospital a top priority, and a child will spend many hours, possibly without food, at the police station. Some kids die there. More die at the hospitals.

"There are still some Korean-American children, but now they are mostly older children. Because these children are so rejected, many social workers will follow a mixed child home if they see one in the streets. They'll try to persuade the mothers to place them in an orphanage, rather than raise them. They usually have success. At one home I visited, the mother said she was keeping her boy only because she expected his father to come someday and take him to America. She had married another full-blooded Korean, and together they had had a daughter. The man would have nothing to do with the older boy, who would refer to him as 'father of my stepsister.' She let her boy be put in a foster home for mixed boys."

At last it was time to go. The two social workers and their twelve young charges boarded the plane for the trip, which would last up to thirty-six hours. At about the same time, the Jeffersons and their two children were driving to New York from their home to meet the flight their daughter would be on. They were leaving a day early because of a snow warning. "We wanted to be sure we'd get there on time. That was the longest day of our lives, waiting and waiting and waiting. There were three other families there too, and we talked a bit, but we were all so nervous."

Carol didn't sleep during the long flight, but she doesn't mind. "Those kids were all so sweet, and looked so cute all sitting in six rows of that huge 747 jet. All the babies were propped up with pillows, and there were only a couple of messy diapers. The only hard part was when we had to take everyone through immigration, but the stewardesses helped carry babies. Sometimes a passenger would offer to feed somebody, so we all did very well. For me the most gratifying part of the experience was handing the kids to the parents. Even though they had never seen them before, most of the parents would just look at a baby and say, 'He's mine.' "

The Jeffersons: "All of a sudden, there was the plane, and after all the other passengers were off, two young women came down the stairs, each holding one baby and leading a small child by the hand. There was a social worker at the airport with us, and we tried to restrain our excitement because she seemed so calm, but it was almost impossible. We recognized our little girl, but waited until the small baby was given to another family. We must have looked quite silly to the other passengers, standing there holding a giant panda bear. We didn't run because we were afraid we'd scare her, and at last the escort brought her over and we picked her up and she smiled. Everything else is a blur."

Carol: "I remember two children in particular. One was a nine-year-old girl. Being so much older than the other children, the strangeness was very frightening to her. She cried several times, and would look at the pictures of her foster brothers and sisters she had taken with her. (Each child had a small sack with a few special belongings.) Her new parents seemed just as confused as she was, and I worried about them for several days after I got back. Finally, I called to see how they were doing. The little girl had moped for several days because everything was so strange. They had finally contacted a family who had also adopted an older Korean child, and the two girls had played together a few times. Both she and her new parents were perking up, and things seemed to be getting better.

"The other child was a little girl about three. I had seen her at the orphanage where she lived, and she was a happy little thing, but on the flight she never smiled once. She wasn't unhappy, just very serious. She held my hand tightly when we arrived, and was still very serious. We walked up to her family at the airport and her new father just picked her up in his arms and gave her a huge, stuffed bear, and she grinned from ear to ear."

In addition to the children in the United States who need families, there are countless thousands of homeless children in countries scattered around the globe. Americans have adopted Korean children since the Korean War, and several agencies work to bring children here from that country. The war in Vietnam has furthered interest in overseas adoption, and Vietnamese children are beginning to come over to the United States also.

No doubt one reason for the popularity of international adoption is the shortage of white babies. Couples anxious for "only a baby" are able to adopt a foreign baby more easily, since there are more of them. As more couples decide to adopt them, the waiting period increases too. A family interested in a Korean baby in 1970 may have had to wait only five or six months. In January, 1973, some agencies forecast at least a two-year wait.

The desire to adopt foreign children, mainly Korean and Vietnamese, is not limited to babies. Older children are adopted as well. While it is easy to understand why a childless couple will prefer a baby, any baby, to an American older child, many parents and social workers are puzzled when a couple will ignore older children in American foster care in favor of the foreign child. They point out how little a family knows about the foreign child, and how much greater the risk can be in terms of health and emotional problems. The number of children needing homes in their own state may be one reason some adoption agencies don't place foreign children.

Usually parents feel that the need in these other countries is so much greater; that American children in foster care have life infinitely better. While this may be their sincere feeling, it does not satisfy the skeptics. Because this issue does concern so many families, we thought we'd mention some theories of our own.

First is what we have heard referred to as the "China doll" myth – "All Oriental kids are cute, while American kids can be homely." People who feel this way disregard the fact that any child can be homely, and that being cute is no guarantee of a happy, adjusted child. They are probably more tolerant of whatever problems "cute" children may have, than of those of a child whom they do not find so attractive.

Second, while parents realize that older children have formed personalities, they also want these foreign children to reflect some of their ideals and viewpoints. American children in foster care are part of our culture – have definite opinions on all aspects of life, racial, cultural, economic, political and social. Foreign children, on the other hand, invariably learn all they know about America from their new parents. This "whole new life" is something some parents feel they alone can give these children. There is a subtle missionary attitude at work.

It is not at all uncommon to hear a person say, "Oh, I want to adopt a Vietnamese child. Look at what we've done to those people." That's not a good reason for adoption. You don't adopt a child because of guilt. You adopt a child because you want to love him or her and be his or her parent.

Many international adoptions are transracial adoptions. All that we say in other places about transracial adoption applies here. Most important, of course, is feeling proud of your child, his racial and national heritage, making him feel this pride, and sharing in it yourself.

There will be many adjustment problems. Agencies provide information on easing the transition but here are some things we would like to emphasize.

1. The language barrier will take a long time to overcome fully. You can ease this difficulty somewhat by trying

to master simple phrases in the child's native language prior to his arrival. Being able to communicate in his own tongue will help put a youngster at ease.

2. The food will be strange. Often these children have had subsistence diets – high in starch, low in protein. While you may take delight in the prospect of restoring health to your new child, you also can't expect him to eat the new foods right away. A gradual change will be better, both for his digestive tract and his mental health. Try and learn what he may have eaten before his arrival, and then have some rice or whatever on hand. Also, don't expect a child who's never seen a knife or fork to be able to use one.

3. Possessions are usually unfamiliar to overseas children, and they are apt to be totally baffled by lots of toys, or even a bed. If your child is more comfortable curled up in a blanket on the floor, let him sleep there. He'll eventually make it to the bed. Don't overwhelm him with toys; he won't know what they are. Let him have one or two things to enjoy and appreciate before he is familiar with our sometimes overmaterialistic culture.

4. Expect some disorientation at first, especially with older children. In addition to strange language, food and lifestyle, they have a time change and often a seasonal change to adjust to. Think how you'd feel if that happened to you.

5. Children from overseas may be excessively polite. They will do as they're told, and seem very well disciplined and independent. They are. Institutional life has taught them that they have to wait their turn and do things on their own in order to survive. Sometimes they do not behave like children at all, but like little mechanical men.

Eventually this behavior will relax, and they will learn to be children again.

6. Young children may not exhibit such "good manners." They may be quite stubborn, in order to get their own way, or even engage in petty thievery. This too is the product of institutional existence, where only the strongest will survive. One hospital Carol Thorp visited had a 30 percent mortality rate, and the foster homes had a 3 to 8 percent mortality rate. Where food, clothing, toys and adult companionship are scarce, children learn to persist and fend for themselves.

7. Many of the children adopted from other countries are old enough to go to school. However, you should not rush them into school in this country. Their life has changed enough for one year. When they are secure in their homes and have mastered the language, it is time enough for schooling. What they need the first year is love and affection and no unnecessary challenges.

8. Health problems are common when children come from another country. Since American immigration rules are more strict than those of other countries about health requirements, many parents think a healthy child will arrive. Instead, adoptions are often delayed while a child is "fattened up" enough to pass through immigration. Nevertheless, some children do arrive with pneumonia, parasites, malnutrition and any number of other problems, so make a visit to a physician a top priority as soon as your child arrives.

9. There are two major sets of rules: those of the United States Immigration and Naturalization Service and those of the governments of the foreign countries involved.

We will not try to explain them, since they are complicated, tend to change from time to time and are different from country to country. Anyone contemplating an overseas adoption should contact a child welfare agency in their area that deals with one of the major international adoption organizations and should consult their local office of the United States Immigration and Naturalization Service.

International adoption is growing. From June, 1970, to June, 1972, there was a 48 percent increase in children coming to the United States for purposes of adoption. The major part of the increase has occurred with children from Korea (from 711 in fiscal year 1970 to 1,374 in 1972) and Vietnam (from 74 in fiscal 1970 to 106 in 1972).[1]

Only four United States–based agencies are directly involved in international adoption. They are the Holt Adoption Program in Creswell, Oregon, the most active of the groups; Travelers' Aid–International Social Service of America in New York City; Welcome House in Doylestown, Pennsylvania; and Lutheran Social Services of Minneapolis, Minnesota. These agencies have representatives in the foreign countries who deal directly with orphanages, child welfare agencies and the governments of those countries in order to locate children needing homes and to make all the necessary paperwork and legal arrangements for the adoption.

The other American agencies have chosen not to get directly involved with international adoption because of its complex nature — all the detailed and sometimes frustrating requirements of the foreign government, the burden of locating the children, and the need for direct contact with parent groups in the United States in order to find homes for the children and support for adoptive parents. Then there's the task of completing home studies on prospective parents, and meeting all immigration and naturalization requirements, and the inevitable pressure from politicians and parents to complete adoptions as a result of the shortage of babies in this country. In addition, many agencies are reluctant to risk being responsible for the child once he is in the country, should the adoption not work out.

The attitude of foreign countries toward releasing their children for adoption varies greatly. Germany, England, Iran, Taiwan, Hong Kong, the Philippines and Canada allow their children to find homes in other countries. Thailand used to permit international adoption, but now feels that its children should remain there. The newly independent countries of Africa have always taken the view that none of their children should be allowed to be adopted in another country. Their pride and sense of nationalism run deep. Latin American countries are reluctant to allow children to leave.

In recent years, both South Korea and South Vietnam, which participate in adoption with America and some European countries, have been criticized by their northern counterparts for not properly solving their social problems. The existence of many homeless children is pointed to as a failure of their governmental systems.

We hope that strident nationalism and political propaganda do not result in closing off international adoption without, at the same time, developing social welfare programs in the poorer countries to guarantee a decent life for the thousands of orphaned children.

SOME HISTORY AND LEGAL CONTROVERSY

16/ The History and Nature of Adoption

Adoption, as we have known it in the United States for the past hundred years, has been intended to serve the interests of orphans and other children in danger of growing up without a family. Before the establishment of this modern concept of adoption, such a child was at the mercy of whoever took him in. The legal system gave him no help in enforcing any obligations which his "adoptive" parents should have toward him. He was, in a very real sense, at a disadvantage as compared with a biological child. The "adoptive" parents, too, were at a disadvantage. They were reluctant to provide informally a permanent home for a child under the threat that the biological parents, relatives or legal guardian would reassert their legal powers and take the child away.

Today, adoption is the establishment of a new, complete legal relationship of parent and child. It cannot take place unless the child's biological parents (the mother only, if the child is born out of wedlock) or legal guardian consents to it. If the child is twelve years of age or older, most states require his consent as well.

Any pre-existing relationship between a parent and child united by the biological processes of conception and birth is legally ended by an adoption. Sometimes a court will sever a relationship even without parental consent if the parent has failed to meet his responsibilities to the child and if an adoption is in the child's best interests.

The adopted child's rights vis-à-vis his parents are the same as those of the biological child – to inheritance, to support and to the family name.

How does our present-day American view of adoption compare with adoption throughout the course of history and in other cultures?

The belief in the superiority of the biological family is not a universally held one among human societies. Margaret Mead tells us that among the Arapesh, children are often "lent out" to this relative or that friend for weeks at a time when they are only a few years old: "This means that a child learns to think of the world as filled with parents, not merely a place in which all of his safety and happiness depends upon the continuance of his relationship to his own particular parents." [1]

In the Mundugumor tribe, not only are the biological parents not considered to be superior to adoptive ones, but there is a feeling of hostility between father and son and between mother and daughter. A husband is not happy about his wife's pregnancy. Unhappily, the women of this society have a strong tendency toward twin births. When such a birth occurs, one of the twins is customarily adopted.[2]

There are also societies in which adoption is the rule and not the exception. In the culture of the Polynesian Marquesas Islands, practically all children are adopted. When a baby is a few months old, the biological parents turn him over to adoptive parents who had requested him even before he was born. The biological parents relinquish all rights to their child and give the adoptive parents a substantial gift in recognition of the expense they will have to bear in raising the child!

Historically, adoption has not always been intended to serve the best interests of children. The social and legal goals of one civilization or culture are not necessarily those of another. Our view of the major purpose of adoption – to provide a permanent family for a child in need of love and security – has only recently been generally accepted as one of prime importance.

Primitive tribes used the idea of adoption in order to combine peacefully with one another on a basis of equality. Some ancient civilizations engaged in adoption in order to assure the continuation of the custom of ancestor worship. The ancient Chinese deemed ancestor worship so important that they established the custom whereby a childless male was entitled to claim the firstborn male child of his younger brothers. The importance of perpetuation of the family to the Babylonians – and the relative unimportance of the psychological well-being of the child – is shown by the following section of the Code of Hammurabi, some four thousand years old:

> If a man take a child in his name, adopt him as a son, this grownup son may not be demanded back.

If a man adopt a child as his son, and after he has taken him, he transgresses against his foster father, that adopted son shall return to the house of his own father.[3]

According to the Bible, adoption did occasionally serve the interests of homeless children. Pharaoh's daughter discovered an abandoned baby in a basket among the bullrushes: ". . . and she adopted him for a son, and called him Moses, saying: Because I took him out of the water." [4]

It was in the Roman Empire, however, where the practice of adoption became popular and where the foundation of modern adoption law was laid. The purposes were both social and religious. The father in early Roman society had complete authority over his children and descendants, even the power of life and death. This dominance had a crucial effect on the development of adoption, for it resulted in the Roman notion that the adopted child, like the biological child, was completely subject to his new father. All ties with the biological family were cut – legal, economic and religious. Once an adoption was formalized, there was no possibility of undoing it. The adopted child became part of the family of the adoptive father. He was, therefore, in a position to satisfy the two major purposes of the adoption: to continue the adopter's family, and to perpetuate the family's religious rites of worship.

Thus, even though adoption in the Roman Empire was not intended to serve the child's interests, the complete severance of all relationships between the child and the biological family and the complete joining of relationships between the child and his adoptive family formed the basis for the development of the modern law of adoption.

Unfortunately for the interests of adopted children, the United States drew its legal traditions not from the Roman or "civil" law, but, rather, from the English or "common" law. And in England, the legal procedure of adoption did not even exist until 1926. The major reason for this lack was that the feudal traditions of England dictated that the rights and property of a parent could pass only to biological children born during wedlock. A child who was born out of wedlock, or who otherwise became part of a family, would never be considered an heir.

At times the injustice of this system caused the English courts to construct some absurd legal fictions in order to allow a particular child to inherit, even though he in fact was not related by blood. In one case, a sailor went to sea for a period of three years shortly after his marriage. One month before he returned, his wife gave birth to a baby. Upon the sailor's death, the child sought to inherit as his heir. The judges decided that the child was in fact an heir because, in their words: ". . . the privities of husband and wife are not to be known, and he might have come by night and engendered the plaintiff [the child]." [5]

The emphasis on blood lineage was the major reason English law failed to provide a process of adoption. Unlike the Romans, the English had no religious motive for perpetuating the family. Moreover, a family's economic and social interests could not be perpetuated through adoption. This was because medieval English society featured elaborate methods for transferring wealth and power which were not necessarily dependent on family relationships – the feudal system of tenure based on landholding.

The English did show some concern for the plight of

children in need of homes and families, although adoption was not chosen as one of the solutions. Rather, the economic organization of England created a substitute – the system of "putting out," or apprenticing, children. From an early age, most English children, and nearly all poor children, left their homes for varying periods of time to live and work with another family. This practice provided opportunities for occupational training and assured that each child would contribute productively to the economic and social structure when he grew older. At the same time, as anyone familiar with the novels of Charles Dickens knows well, the system resulted in cruelty and deprivation. But it was a social alternative for children who were without biological families. The apprenticing system, coupled with the legal tradition discussed above, postponed the recognition of adoption in England until the Adoption of Children Act in 1926.

The legal and social traditions of England were carried over to America. "Putting out" and apprenticeship were common to the Puritans in New England, although their motives were somewhat different from those of the English. As one historian puts it, "Puritan parents did not trust themselves with their own children. . . . They were afraid of spoiling them by too great affection." [6]

The economic development which followed the colonization of America in the seventeenth century drew large numbers of English apprentices for child labor: "The apprenticing of poor children to the Virginia Company began as early as 1620. . . . A record of 1627 reads: 'There are many ships going to Virginia and with them

1400 or 1500 children which they have gathered up in divers places.' "[7]

During the eighteenth and nineteenth centuries, the "putting out" system in America continued. At the same time, a practice much like modern adoption grew without any governmental or legal sanction. Blood relatives began taking responsibility for orphaned and dependent children. And it became common for people to specify in their wills the relative with whom the orphaned child should live. Most likely, the ease with which this custom of adoption developed was due to the emigration of non-English Americans who came from countries where the influence of Roman legal and social tradition was strong, such as France, Italy and other countries in continental Europe.

By the middle of the nineteenth century, the economic and social structure of the United States was changing rapidly. Industrialization and immigration were transforming the country, particularly in the cities. The problems of orphaned, neglected and dependent children completely outstripped the capacity of the "putting out" system and the custom of private adoption to provide homes and families. Child welfare agencies were formed, usually with church sponsorship. They placed these children in "special" institutions or, preferably, in foster and adoptive families.

This vast social effort was not universally accepted. In the words of Reverend Charles Loring Brace, founder of the New York Children's Aid Society:

> It is feared that these children would corrupt the morals of the families to which they are sent. . . . We must remind such

persons [the critics of adoption] of the wonderful capacity for improvement in children's natures under new circumstances; and we assert boldly, that a poor child taken in thus by the hand of Christian charity, and placed in a new world of love and of religion, is *more likely to be tempted to good*, than to tempt others to evil.[8]

We can forgive the Reverend Mr. Brace his overdone attempt to justify adoption, given the tenor of the times. Unfortunately, his paternalistic views are still reflected in attitudes today, when adoption long since should have been considered both common and successful.

A general citizens' movement for reform in child welfare resulted from the problems accompanying America's industrialization and population growth toward the end of the nineteenth century. The establishment of adoption laws was one part of this movement. The first adoption statutes in the United States took the form of "private" laws which permitted an adoption by a specific, named parent of an identified individual child. In 1851, Massachusetts enacted the first law that made the process of adoption open to everyone.

Legislation was required because, as we have seen, our courts could find no sanction for the process in the English common-law system, which supplied the basis for decisions by American courts. Although there is evidence that adoption was practiced by American Indians[9] and native Hawaiians,[10] the judges, educated in the English law, refused to follow customs and traditions indigenous to their own country.

The early laws and judicial interpretations of them show no consistent philosophy and are a far cry from the modern notion that the purpose of adoption is to serve the best interests of the child. A commonly held view was that adopted children were "the waifs of society, foundlings or children whose parents are depraved and worthless." [11] This feeling was combined with "the growing belief that many traits of mind are hereditary and almost irradicable." [12] Children who needed to be adopted were considered inferior. The result was court decisions on the rights of adopted children which favored biological relationships over those formed through adoption. It was only after social concern for homeless children became widespread that adoption law began to recognize the interests of the children.

In addition to the child's interests, there still were those of the biological parents and their families, the prospective adoptive parents and their families, and of society itself. Adoption has become a complicated social and legal process which demands sensitivity on the part of social service agencies, lawyers, judges and legislators. It is not surprising that particular adoptions have served as the focus for clashing social forces and personal interests. The role of our social and legal system should be to minimize the harm that can result from such controversy and assure that the greatest good will be served in the end. We believe that the greatest good must be the welfare of the child.

A century of growth and development of our legal rules and social work profession has been intended to protect the best interests of children. Unfortunately, despite this intent, the rules and procedures in adoption do not yet assure that those interests are paramount.

17/ When the Biological Mother Changes Her Mind

SOME of the most tragic human suffering in adoption occurs when biological parents (usually the mother of a child born out of wedlock) have changed their minds after the child has been placed in an adoptive family, but before the adoption has been finalized in court. In legal terms, this is known as "revocation of consent." The rules which determine the rights of biological parents to do so vary dramatically from state to state; generally, they fall into three categories. Fewer than one-third of the states give the biological parent the absolute right to revoke consent; at least five states make the consent absolutely irrevocable once given in accordance with the law; and all the rest give discretion to the court to determine whether the consent can be withdrawn. That discretion is to be exercised in accordance with the court's view of the best interests of the child.[1]

When parents are permitted to change their minds, it usually hurts the child. Many studies have shown that a permanent, stable family relationship – particularly with a mother figure in the early years – is the most important factor for healthy child development.[2] Yet, we continue to witness adoption cases in which the statutes and the judges seem blind to the effects on the child. One such situation was the nationally publicized "Baby Lenore" case.[3]

Baby Lenore was born in a New York hospital on May 18, 1970, to thirty-three-year-old Olga Scarpetta, an unwed mother from Colombia, South America, who had been educated in the United States. Four days after the birth, Miss Scarpetta placed the child in foster care with the Spence-Chapin Child Welfare agency. Ten days later she consented to adoption and signed the required surrender document. The agency then placed the child with Mr. and Mrs. DeMartino, prospective adoptive parents. Shortly after that placement, Miss Scarpetta decided to change her mind and requested that the agency return her daughter. The agency refused and there followed a long series of legal battles in New York. Eventually the case reached the United States Supreme Court, which refused to overturn a final decision by the highest court of New York directing the DeMartinos to give the child back.

After being the only parents Baby Lenore knew for the eighteen months of her life, the DeMartinos were faced with the prospect of losing "their" child. They refused to give her up and fled as fugitives from justice from New York to Florida to attempt to escape the effect of the judgment of the New York courts. The law of Florida proved more hospitable to the interests of both the De-

Martinos and Baby Lenore. After a long legal fight, they were allowed to adopt the child and live in Florida.

There are many remarkable aspects to this case – the inability of the Spence-Chapin agency to assure the reliability of Miss Scarpetta's surrender, the failure of the agency to notify the DeMartinos of Miss Scarpetta's change of mind, and the extraordinary favoring of the biological parent under New York's statutes. But what is most striking is the diametrically opposite attitude of the New York and Florida courts toward adoptive parents and the process of adoption.

The New York Appellate Court started with an assumption that the biological parent is superior to an adoptive parent. In the court's words:

> . . . the status of a natural parent is so important that in determining the best interest of the child, it may counterbalance, even outweigh, superior material and cultural advantages which may be afforded by adoptive parents. . . . For experience teaches that a mother's love is a factor which will endure; possibly endure after other claimed material advantages and emotional attachments may have proven transient.[4]

The court assumed that the best interests of the child would be served by return to the biological mother so long as she was not clearly unfit. It also assumed that biology is the most important criterion for motherhood. It lightly brushed aside the fact that Miss Scarpetta had surrendered the child, and nowhere did it explain how the best interests of Baby Lenore would be served by the return.

The Florida courts, on the other hand, treated the

interests of Miss Scarpetta as secondary to the overriding issue of the child's best interests. They had no trouble whatsoever in concluding that separation of the child from the only parents she had ever known would be harmful to her, perhaps resulting in permanent psychological damage.

It is time that all courts and legislatures began to consider the best interests of the child in the light of both common sense and modern psychology. An interruption of the established, dependable parent-child relationship can produce trauma and anxiety, which upset the foundation of basic trust that is so crucial to the development of a child's personality.[5] The interruption may well result in permanent emotional harm.

A biological parent may start out with a special emotional attachment to the child which has great potential for a healthy parent-child relationship. However, this potential diminishes once the parent surrenders custody of the child. As soon as the prospective adoptive parents begin to provide the kind of love and warmth essential for the child, the special position of the biological parent is less justifiable. To allow revocation of consent and interruption of the new relationship would be to ignore the best interests of the child.

We believe that allowing biological parents to change their minds once the child has been surrendered in a responsible, carefully considered way is contrary to their best interests also. Laws which permit revocation encourage uncertainty and vacillation. The act of giving up a child is a very traumatic experience and undoubtedly one of the most difficult decisions a person makes in his or her life.

An unwed girl delivering a child when she herself is little more than a child must summon all the courage, sensitivity and maturity she possibly can. She is not helped by a system of laws and procedures which tell her: "Your decision is only temporary; you can always try to get the child back in a few months if you change your mind."

Under that system she isn't likely to take her decision as seriously as she should. The law does her no favor by allowing her the chance to delay or even escape hard choices. When she knows that her decision is final, the process of choosing is more likely to contribute to her personal growth. Laws which permit revocation are as unfair to biological parents as to the child and the prospective adoptive parents.

If the consent for adoption is to be irrevocable, however, we must be sure that it does serve the interests of the biological parent. The procedure for giving consent ought to be consistent with the seriousness of the decision and ought to be such that the parent can fully understand the gravity and permanent nature of what she is doing. At a minimum, states should require a uniform surrender document for all adoptions, such as the one in use in Massachusetts (see Appendix C) and should permit an attorney for the biological parent to be present with at least two witnesses. If practical difficulties which might unnecessarily delay adoptions can be overcome, an even more effective procedure may include having the parent appear before a judge, as recommended by the Children's Bureau of the United States Department of Health, Education and Welfare.

The adoptive family is, as we have observed, keenly and

adversely affected by any possible revocation. No adoptive parent has escaped the feeling of fear that his child might not be his after all. The security he receives when a surrender is irrevocable, though not as important as the interests of the child or the fairness to the biological parents, is a real benefit from that type of procedure.

18/ When an Unwed Father Wants the Child

THE interests of the father of a child born out of wedlock have until recently been ignored by the law. He has had no right to raise his child or even be involved in planning for him. Yet he has been legally responsible for his support and, in some cases, for the medical expenses of the mother as a result of giving birth. When a mother surrendered a child born out of wedlock for adoption, the father has had no more rights than a complete stranger.

Several years ago a child was born to Mr. M. and Miss P. The parents chose not to marry but agreed that the baby would live with Mr. M. and his parents. When the baby was six months old, Miss P. decided to surrender him to an agency for adoption. The agency then sent a worker to remove the baby physically from the home of Mr. M. and the baby's grandparents. The worker, taking advantage of the lack of education of the grandparents, convinced them that they had no right to the baby and succeeded in transferring custody to prospective parents selected by the agency. Mr. M. and his parents were distraught and tried to appeal to the agency to let them continue to raise the baby – they told of their love for him and how they considered him part of the family. They told the agency that their Puerto Rican heritage made them feel very strongly about all their blood relations – including a child born out of wedlock. The baby was part of their family and always would be. Mr. M. pleaded for the chance to be a father to his child and assured the agency that he had a good job and the desire to provide both love and support.

The agency refused to return the child. They said that the law gave rights only to the mother of a child if the parents weren't married, and when the mother agreed to adoption and surrendered the baby, the duty of the agency was to find an adoptive family for it.

Mr. M. continued to fight for his baby. He tried, through his representative in the legislature, to get the state law changed to give the father the right to consent to any adoption petition presented from that time forward. However, there was little legislative support for that proposal because it would have placed in jeopardy hundreds of adoptions which had already been made but not yet finalized. The legislature felt that the price was much too high for the slim chance that a few unwed fathers might be interested in their children.

When the adoptive couple petitioned the court for finalization of the adoption of Mr. M.'s child, he tried to fight it in the courts. But the courts would not remove the child from the adoptive home he had been in for over a year for the sake of an unwed father who had no special rights in the eyes of the law. Mr. M. never even had a chance to show what he could have provided for the child.

Today, Mr. M.'s rights might well be more substantial. The United States Supreme Court decided a case in 1972 which will undoubtedly result in a greater recognition of the unwed father's interests. In *Stanley* v. *Illinois*[1] the court decided that an unwed father had the right to a hearing to present his plan for the child before the state could assume custody of it after the death of the mother. Though it did not specifically deal with adoption, the Supreme Court indicated that its decision might also apply to broaden the unwed father's rights there, too.

Before evaluating what the legal outcome of all this might be, let's ask why the unwed father should have any rights at all.

He has been ignored because of the moral stigma attached to fathering a child out of wedlock. The law gave him no rights, just responsibilities. He was, in a sense, punished for his "immoral" act.

But he wasn't the only one punished. The child suffered too. He was an "illegitimate" child, with all the social, legal and economic discrimination that goes with that label. Among the most important things he was denied was any realistic chance of growing up with his father. He was denied any of the emotional or material advantages he might have received from his biological parent.

Finally, it is hard to deny that a special affinity is usually created between a child and the parent who helped conceive him. Though not all parents feel this affinity, and even some who initially do may never reflect it in any meaningful relationship with the child, the fact remains that it can be a very real and valuable thing. And it may be an advantage for the child because it gives him a better chance for a healthy parent-child relationship than he might otherwise have. Why should the child be denied any chance at that kind of relationship? As the Supreme Court stated: "The private interest here, that of a man in the children he has sired and raised, undeniably warrants deference and, absent a powerful countervailing interest, protection." [2]

Despite the Stanley case, the extent of the father's rights is still unclear. Will he be granted the same right as the mother – the right to consent to any adoption – or will the courts decide that the father's interests should be recognized without going that far? Determining the extent of his interests should depend on what the consequences of granting full rights are for the child.

The practical effect of a legal rule which requires the father's consent would be to delay many, if not all, adoptions. This is true because the father's right would come into play only after the mother had surrendered the child for adoption. At that time, the person or agency receiving the child would have to search out the father in order to obtain his consent. Only in ideal cases will the identity and whereabouts of the father be known and will he be ready to consent. In many situations, there would be uncertainty about who or where the father is and whether he would consent. Under such circumstances, prospective adoptive parents may not want to take the risk of a future legal battle over the child. Agencies would, therefore, avoid placing children until after all the likely legal difficulties have been resolved. The motives of the mother and father could complicate the situation even more. If the relationship between the two is acrimonious, the mother might refuse to surrender a child "just so he can't get it." And an unscrupulous father might use his right to consent as an opportunity for troublemaking or even extortion.

As we have said before, the longer a child goes without permanent placement, the greater the potential damage to his psychological well-being. We believe that granting the father full right to consent (or withhold consent) to adoption would increase the chances for such harm to all children born out of wedlock who may need permanent families through adoption. This is too high a price to pay. Yet those unwed fathers who are interested in their children deserve some recognition, some reasonable chance. And so do their children. The Supreme Court has indicated that the Constitution requires it. What is a reasonable solution?

In order to minimize the threat to the normal process of adoption we would suggest a system which (1) benefits only those fathers whose interest is solely in raising their children and not in withholding consent to adoption, and (2) evaluates that interest as soon as possible after the mother surrenders the child. The father would register his interest in gaining permanent custody of the child with some public agency, either the department of public welfare or the courts, prior to the time the mother consents to adoption or within a very short time thereafter. When the child is surrendered, the agency or person receiving him would have to consult the registry and notify the father that the mother has given up the child. The father would then have a short period of time during which to ask a court to grant him custody; he would have to convince a judge that his plan would be in the child's best interests.

This procedure would give the unwed father limited rights – less substantial than those of the mother. He would not have the right to consent – only the right to be heard for his permanent plan for the child. Not all unwed fathers would be recognized – only those who take the initiative and responsibility to be aware of the existence of the child, and who have the desire to raise the child in the event of the mother's surrender. The time for making the interest known would be made quite short in order to avoid unnecessary delay in finding the child a home.

We believe that these limits on the rights of the father are justified in light of the overriding rights of the child to a permanent family situation as early in his life as possible. Broader rights at present would significantly hinder providing families through adoption for children who need them. And broader rights are not really necessary in order to give a fair opportunity to those fathers who really care about their children.

19/ When Biological Parents Abuse, Neglect or Abandon the Child

NOT all children who are adopted have been voluntarily given up by their biological parents. Some have been abused, neglected or abandoned, forcing a court judgment that all the rights of the parent should be ended. Most states have laws which permit the involuntary termination of parental rights when the parent has failed to carry out the basic responsibilities of parenthood and when, in the court's view, the best interests of the child warrant such action. Despite the availability of this legal procedure, courts are very reluctant to interfere with parental control. There exists a general predisposition to favor the parent, even though the law and common sense say the best interests of the child should prevail. Perhaps because the American legal system was inherited largely from the English common law, with its emphasis on property rights and blood ties, American courts often speak of a presumption in favor of a parent's fitness.[1] That presumption often works against the best interests of the child by delaying his chance for a stable, loving parent-child relationship in another home.

A typical case would be the following.

Mr. and Mrs. Smith were married when she was seventeen, he twenty. Neither of them has any specialized vocational training. Mr. Smith works as a house painter, Mrs. Smith as a domestic. Soon after their marriage, Mrs. Smith becomes pregnant and stops working. After the birth of the baby, whom they name Bobby, Mr. Smith becomes jealous and begins to spend more and more time away from home. Mrs. Smith finds caring for Bobby a difficult job and becomes more and more depressed because of the lack of support from her husband. Bad economic times put Mr. Smith out of work and he begins to drink heavily. After many violent arguments, Mrs. Smith tells her husband to leave the house, which he does, and she tries to find a job, leaving the now three-year-old Bobby alone part of the day. Unable to find work, Mrs. Smith sometimes takes out her frustration on Bobby by beating him. A neighbor reports the case to the state department of welfare, who investigate and offer counseling, which Mrs. Smith refuses. Several weeks later, Bobby is rushed to the emergency room at the local hospital after receiving severe cuts and bruises from his latest beating. This time the department of welfare petitions a court to transfer custody of the child to it in order to prevent further abuse and to place Bobby in foster care. The judge grants the petition and suggests that Mrs. Smith seek professional therapy. She promises she will.

Bobby is placed in a foster home with six other children. The worker from the department is supposed to work with Mrs. Smith and Bobby in an attempt to get the family back together, but in fact the staff shortage in the department is so acute that all she has time to do is visit Bobby once each month.

Mrs. Smith at first manages to see her son every week, but as her psychological condition deteriorates, visits become less frequent. After three months in foster care, Bobby has to be moved to a second foster home because the first foster mother has become ill and can no longer care for seven children. The second foster home is located over forty miles from the city in which the Smiths live, because the department has great difficulty in finding nearby foster homes for children who need special attention. Bobby has begun to show signs of retardation and needs a good deal of time on a one-to-one basis. Mrs. Smith manages to visit him during his first month at the new foster home but ceases to visit thereafter. Six months after Bobby has entered this second home, the agency worker confers with her supervisor about the case.

The second foster parents, Mr. and Mrs. Johnson, have asked the worker if they can adopt Bobby, since Mrs. Johnson spends more time with him than any of her own children and has grown to love him very much. She feels that he really isn't retarded, but just needs a lot of love and security to get over his frightening experiences with his mother. The supervisor decides that it is too soon to think of adoption and asks the worker to try harder to involve Mrs. Smith.

The worker repeatedly attempts to help Mrs. Smith and to get her to visit Bobby, but she has no interest in him any longer and is busy trying to divorce her husband in order to marry her boyfriend, who has been pressuring her to give the child up for adoption.

Months pass and the only contact Bobby has with his family is a Christmas card from his father, who is a patient in a state mental health hospital.

When the boy is four and a half years old – fifteen months after arriving at the Johnsons', Mr. Johnson is told he is being transferred to another state by his company. His wife frantically calls the welfare department and pleads with the supervisor to do what she can to allow her and her husband to adopt Bobby before they are transferred. They cannot bear to part with him. The supervisor finally agrees to get Mr. and Mrs. Smith to consent to the adoption. However, Mr. Smith's doctors feel that he is not legally competent to give consent, and Mrs. Smith refuses to give consent, at least not before getting her divorce.

The agency then has to decide whether to ask a court to terminate the rights of Mr. and Mrs. Smith involuntarily. The legal advisor to the agency states that the history of child abuse, coupled with the absence of meaningful contact with the boy for over a year, should make a persuasive case, but cautions that it all depends on the discretion of the individual judge in determining the best interests of the child. The decision is made to go to court.

Due to the backlog of cases, the hearing on Bobby's case is scheduled for three months after the initial decision to bring the adoption petition. Mrs. Smith, after receiving notice that the agency wants Bobby freed for adoption without her consent, decides to contest the case. Mr. Smith and his guardian does not.

Through her publicly supported lawyer, Mrs. Smith requests and receives a two-month delay in the hearing so that he might have time to prepare his case. When the hearing is finally held, the department of welfare calls several witnesses to show that the Smiths had neglected and, in effect, abandoned Bobby. They also are required to show why the termination of the right to consent to adoption would be in his best interests. That is, they must persuade the judge that adoption at the time is both possible and desirable. Mrs. Smith, on the other hand, merely tells the judge that she still considers Bobby her son and that she hopes sometime soon to be able to take him back.

The judge decides not to terminate the parental rights, but leaves the child in the custody of the department of welfare for six months in order to see whether Mrs. Smith can improve her situation sufficiently to assume parental responsibility.

Putting off any permanent decision has unfortunate results. The Johnsons have had to move out of state and Bobby is placed in his third foster home in less than two years. The separation has regressive effects on his emotional and intellectual development. The third foster family, though well-meaning, is entirely untrained and ill-equipped to handle Bobby's emotional trauma or his special needs. Once more, he appears retarded and increasingly unable to get along in the public school kindergarten class. Beyond that, his emotional problems go untreated – first because the foster family has no understanding of them, and second, because there are no conveniently located community-based mental health treatment resources.

When the department and Mrs. Smith appear before the court six months later, Bobby's needs have become much more acute, yet Mrs. Smith's capacity and willingness to assume responsibility have not changed. This time, the department tells the judge that they feel it is Bobby's last chance at adoption – that he is probably headed for an institution rather soon unless a stable, understanding family with appropriate supportive services can be found for him. Even if the boy were freed for adoption, the department says, an extraordinary effort would have to be made to find suitable parents.

The judge decides that the time has come to terminate the rights of Mr. and Mrs. Smith, and he issues an order doing so. This time he is convinced that it is in Bobby's best interests.

Unfortunately, parents like the Johnsons, Bobby's second foster family, are not readily available. He was not placed until he was almost six years old and the many emotional and intellectual needs which resulted from his chaotic early life remained with him throughout childhood.

The attitudes shown in Bobby's story are exhibited every day, to the detriment of thousands of children. The reluctance of the legal system to end the relationship of parent and child; the inability of a biological parent to let go of his child, even after he has ceased being a parent in any meaningful sense of the word; the vacillation of the child welfare agency in making decisions about freeing children for adoption; and the failure of temporary care provided under the auspices of such agencies, particularly the public agencies conducting large foster care programs, all hurt the children. There is a crying need for a change in public attitudes and for clear legislative standards on ending parental rights. Those attitudes and standards should be based on the well-being of children. After all, a child's "right" to loving and responsible parents ought to be more important than the parent's "right" to withhold consent to adoption! A child is not a piece of property which a parent can decide to buy or sell. He is a person whose development can be seriously damaged by abuse, neglect and abandonment.

There are thousands of children like Bobby who are now in foster care, in institutions, or being victimized by abusive parents. For them, adoption holds great promise, but only if social workers, lawyers, judges and the general public begin to look upon parenthood as something to be earned and constantly merited. Only then will the laws now on the books and any new ones which are passed be effective in protecting the best interests of each and every child.

20/ When There Are Religious Restrictions

Is IT important to you that a baby be adopted only by parents of the same religion as that of the biological mother? Or that atheists be forbidden the opportunity to adopt at all?

Is it better for a child to live in an institution or in foster care than to be adopted early in life by a family with the "wrong" religion or of mixed religion?

Does a child have religion as soon as he is born?

Is membership in a particular church or synagogue as important as living an ethical and moral life?

These are all questions whose answers usually reflect strong opinions. Not many people are neutral about them.

When legislatures, courts and agencies adhere to legal restrictions on adoption based on religion, they answer all these questions in the affirmative.

The question we pose is: How have these restrictions affected the lives of children needing families?

In one famous Massachusetts case [1] the prospective parents in an independent adoption were given two-week-old twins directly from the hospital where they were born. The couple, Mr. and Mrs. Goldman, was Jewish; the biological mother was Catholic. The court-ordered investigation concluded that the Goldmans were fine people and provided a warm, loving home for the children. However, the courts refused to grant the petition for adoption because the law at that time was interpreted to mean that children may not be adopted by parents of a different religion from that of the biological mother. The only way an adoption could legally cross religious lines was if there were no parents available of the required religious faith – a highly unlikely prospect.

The court in this and similar cases was completely indifferent to the fact that the twins were almost four years old when the case was finally decided. They had known no other parents than the Goldmans. The psychological damage to them, and the hurt and anguish to all concerned, was coldly brushed aside.

Prospective adoptive couples involved in cases like this have been known to pack up all their belongings, sell house and business, and leave the state in order to escape the effect of the court decree. In one case [2] the couple was subject to kidnapping charges – a felony punishable by life imprisonment. However, the governor of the state to which they fled refused to authorize their extradition. The courts in that state later approved the adoption even though an official representative of the home state tried to persuade the courts not to do so. Although the case had a happy ending, the adoptive family suffered terribly through the entire process.

Laws based on religious restrictions cause child welfare agencies to limit the parents they serve and to decrease the opportunities for children who need family life. Such laws also increase the likelihood of non-agency-sponsored adoptions. Prospective parents whose particular religion, or lack of religion, would inhibit their chances for receiving a child through an agency, often seek other opportunities through private sources. Their desire for children is only made more desperate.

Is there any justification for these laws? Their purpose is to match the religion of the adoptive parents and the child. People in favor of them say that a child should be placed in a home with parents of the same religious belief as his biological mother. They believe that religion is more relevant than any other factor in determining whether an adoption should take place.

Many states have relaxed such restrictions in recent years and broadened the discretion of the courts. However, heartache and tragedy has resulted and continues to result in the name of this principle.

Sometimes, restrictive laws can be interpreted in light of the best interests of the child. In a New York case, for example, a biological mother tried to get back her son, whom she had surrendered four years previously, on the grounds that he was Catholic and the adoptive parents were Protestant. The law was the same as that in the Massachusetts cases mentioned above: "The court shall when practicable . . . give custody . . . only to . . . persons of the same religious faith as that of the child." However, the New York court approved the adoption, stating:

> The statute may not be employed as a means of wiping out a relationship . . . which . . . has continued for the entire four and a half years of the youngster's life. . . . If the rule were otherwise, the [adoptive] parents would ever run the risk of not being able to adopt the child, and the child ever subjected to the danger of having attachments formed painfully severed. . . .[3]

This court put religion in perspective and considered the overall well-being of the child. That, after all, is supposed to be the purpose of child welfare laws and social service agencies. In fact, the modern trend in interpreting these restrictive laws is to honor them only when the best interests of the child will not be compromised.

It has been only in the past few decades that religion has been thought to be so important. Before that it was common for courts in adoption cases to consider the total child rather than one aspect of his background or lifestyle. In 1907, the Massachusetts Supreme Judicial Court came directly to the point:

> The first and paramount duty is to consult the welfare of the child. The wishes of the parent as to the religious education and surroundings of the child are entitled to weight; if there is nothing to put in the balance against them, ordinarily they will be decisive. If, however, those wishes cannot be carried into effect without sacrificing what the court sees to be for the welfare of the child, they must so far be disregarded.[4]

Given these older principles, you might ask why in the world they were ever departed from. The answer is that state legislatures passed restrictive laws because politically powerful interests wanted them passed. Those interests were largely the Irish, Italian, Polish and other primarily Catholic immigrant groups in the urban states and the Catholic Church itself. To some degree, the laws were a reaction to the practice of wealthy, Protestant families and child welfare agencies, which consisted of taking in and later adopting neglected, abandoned or merely "illegitimate" children of women from immigrant, Catholic families. These women and children were the victims of poverty, lack of opportunity and public intolerance.

The laws were intended as much to improve and protect the status of the Catholic religion as they were to preserve any parental right to control religious upbringing or to assure the welfare of the child. One judge in Massachusetts put it this way: "I find that no one, not even the parents [biological], have the right to deny an immature child who has been baptized a Roman Catholic the privilege of being reared in Catholicity." [5] Another in New York agreed and went so far as to prefer institutionalization:

> . . . it was and still is practicable to give these infants to an institution under the control of persons of their religious faith. . . . To this the children have a natural and legal right of which they cannot be deprived by their temporary exposure to the culture of another religion prior to the age of reason.[6]

Even where the biological mother specifically consents to a different religious upbringing, courts have refused to cross religious lines.[7] This type of decision means that a child should be brought up in the religion to which he was born – not so much because the child will suffer if he isn't – but because the value of the religion is thought so great that the child is entitled to remain part of it. This corresponds with the principle of the Roman Catholic religion that "Catholic baptism is immutable and accordingly there is no exit from the Catholic faith." [8]

It is not surprising, then, that religious restrictions in adoption have at times been openly fought for by representatives of the Roman Catholic Church. The following excerpt from the official newspaper of the diocese of Brooklyn reports on such activity in Pennsylvania:

> A new [Pennsylvania] state child adoption bill was passed by the legislature and sent to the Governor for signature after a Senate-House conference had amended the measure to eliminate features condemned – and include others advocated – by Pennsylvania Catholic leaders.[9]

In a similar manner, efforts to remove religious restrictions have been openly fought against by Catholic spokesmen.[10]

Church doctrine shows signs of changing in the face of several factors crucial to the welfare of the adoptive child, particularly the need to avoid delay in placement in a permanent home and the greater difficulty in finding homes for children considered "hard to place." Moreover, there is little logical religious objection to the transreligious placement of a child who has not as yet been baptized, as is the case with many children surrendered soon after birth.

Many people believe that a parent has a right to determine his child's religion. But should this right extend to a parent who surrenders his child for adoption? We believe that the best interests of the child require that parents surrender *all* rights to the child as soon as consent to adoption is given. But even if the right to choose the child's religion extended to the biological parent, can that possibly justify a law which prevents a transreligious adoption when the parent consents to one?

What about the situation in which the biological mother and father are of different religions – why should that of the mother be arbitrarily taken as the one to prevail?

And what of situations in which the parent himself practices no religion but was born of parents who did?

Finally, there is no justification for the common practice of assigning religious affiliations to a child merely because he was abandoned or there is dispute over what his parents' religion really is. Many ridiculous fictions have been perpetrated in order to comply with laws which require such identification, such as affiliating with a church or synagogue long enough to adopt a child and then resigning.

Sometimes religious restrictions are defended on the grounds that the adoptive process ought to "match" parents with child. This was clearly the feeling of one judge when he observed:

> The mother did not cease to be a Catholic even if she did not live up to the ideals of her religion. . . . The petitioners are of the Jewish faith and intend to bring up the twins in that faith. . . . The petitioners have dark complexions and dark hair. The twins are blond, with large blue eyes and flaxen hair.[11]

It is natural for parents to want their children – biological or adopted – to reflect some of their "better" qualities. However, we believe that this concern for matching, when carried to an extreme, might indicate a refusal to accept an adopted child as just as good as a biological child.

It is up to social workers and prospective adoptive parents to talk out such feelings fully.

What can be said against these religious restrictions?

First of all, they are inconsistent with the basic purpose of adoption laws – to provide a permanent family for a child who needs one. This purpose can be frustrated as a child waits until a family with the "right" religion is found. During that period of delay, the child could be institutionalized or moved from foster home to foster home.

In a landmark study for the World Health Organization, Sir John Bowlby stated that ". . . the evidence . . . points unmistakenly to its being in the best interests of an adopted baby's mental health for him to be adopted soon after birth." [12]

Emphasis on the religious factor can also prevent bringing a child together with a family which would be particularly suited to his needs. This is important for handicapped, retarded, or emotionally disturbed children. Automatically decreasing the pool of prospective parents cheats the children far more than it deprives those excluded from parenthood.

We question whether laws should give support to the parochial idea that the "status" of being part of a particular religion is important. That idea is inconsistent with the traditions of America, where believers and nonbelievers are treated equally.

Laws making religion the prime factor in adoption have no relationship to the interests of the people actually involved in an adoption. For children who have been living happily in an adoptive home, such laws are the cause of great tragedy. For others, who may languish in foster care, they cruelly close off opportunities for a permanent family. For the majority of biological and prospective adoptive parents to whom religion is not of prime importance, they are, at best, irrelevant, and, at worst, a guilt-producing nuisance. For most agencies and courts they force a struggle to find ways to avoid strict interpretations.

Sectarian agencies are available to those parents who do consider religion of prime importance. There, a biological parent can make his or her wishes known and an adoptive couple can request a child with a particular background.

When religion is important to the child – as in the case of an older child who has experienced religious training and practices a particular faith, agencies and courts have ample discretion to give special recognition to the religious factor.

The modern trend in law and in social work is to treat religion as one of many factors relevant to an adoption, with any specific request of the biological parent to be balanced against the best interests of the child.[13] There remains the danger, however, that a given judge, or social worker, or state legislature will deviate from the trend and fall back on traditional patterns and prejudices. As recently as November, 1970, a court in New Jersey refused to allow an adoption sponsored by a child welfare agency and consented to by biological parents solely because the prospective adoptive couple did not profess a belief in a conventional religion.[14] Although the judge admitted that the couple were "persons of high ethical and moral standards," he felt that their lack of religion as he defined it would prejudice the child's "right" to believe in God. The fact that the couple had successfully raised an older child adopted under the auspices of the same agency and had been fine parents for the girl in question for the year and one half of her life meant nothing. This decision provoked an editorial in the New York *Times* denouncing the attempt to force religious identification upon the child.[15] The case was subsequently reversed by a higher court, which indicated that it may even be unconstitutional to deny the opportunity for adoption to persons solely because of their lack of belief in established religion.[16]

Some states have new laws which, in very clear language, assure that the religious factor is not given undue weight in any particular case.[17] Political action in the rest of the country will be necessary in order to prevent even one more tragic case.

EPILOGUE

21/ The Future of Adoption

We know that the main purpose of adoption is to bring adults and children together into loving families.

We also know that adoption is no longer restricted to childless couples and white, healthy babies. Agencies have started to take the "radical" step of placing formerly "unadoptable" children in families. And prospective parents have seen beyond their own physical appearance and traditional value system to appreciate the needs of all children.

We have listened to many prospective parents complain about the long, and often futile, wait for a healthy baby. Infertile couples, especially, feel a deep sadness when they are told that their desire for the child of their choice cannot be satisfied. We understand their disappointment and empathize with them. At the same time, the present baby shortage is a welcome sign that fewer unwanted births are occurring. Increased use of contraceptives and the rise in abortions are (undoubtedly) having an impact on adoption trends.

No longer can adoption be thought of primarily as a means for childless couples to begin their families.

And no longer will adoption primarily serve the newborn baby.

The future of adoption will lie in providing permanent families for the children who are in limbo – those who are unwanted because they have special needs; those who languish in foster care; those who are the victims of institutions; and those who have been relegated to a life of insecurity because faceless people have decided that they were "unadoptable."

The future of adoption should also involve a worldwide effort to bring countless ostracized children orphaned by poverty and war together with loving and responsible families, no matter what their nationality, color, religion or political system.

We see four specific developments which we feel have the potential of mobilizing all the resources necessary to find homes for the children who will need them and to educate the public about the naturalness of adoption. They are the adoptive parents' organizations, the adoption resource exchange, publicity in the mass media, and United Nations involvement. We'd like to share them with you.

The Adoptive Parents' Organizations

Very early in our personal adoptive experience, we found out about the existence of adoptive parents' groups. We were able to learn about different types of adoption, receive advice and discuss adoption with people who had themselves become adoptive families. They had a candidness social workers couldn't match, and we felt able to talk with them without fear of appearing foolish in front of someone who would judge our ability to be good parents.

These groups are important not only to prospective parents but also to the general public and to the children who wait for families. They serve as an information and referral resource for families interested in adoption. They do volunteer work at agencies, and they work to open dialogue between prospective parents and professional social workers. Various members concentrate on particular areas of adoption which interest them. At the present time some members are turning their attention to adoption of children from Vietnam in order to inform the public, to persuade agencies to get involved, and to pressure the United States government to take a more active role with the government of South Vietnam. Several bills in the 93rd Congress of the United States which seek to aid children in Vietnam and encourage international adoption were filed as a result of action by parents' groups.

No matter what the issue – whether it be the rights of adopted children, religious restrictions on adoption, or fairness of agency policy – legislative and administrative reforms will depend on the existence of "pressure groups." Adoptive parents' organizations can be a powerful and effective advocate for the children who will benefit from adoption.

These groups have been established in many states, in Canada and several other countries. They keep in touch with one another through newsletters and occasional conferences. Three have already been held on transracial adoption and one on international adoption. We have included a list of the groups in the United States and Canada in Appendix A.

Anyone wishing to start a group in an area not already served might begin by contacting one or more existing groups for their advice. Child welfare agencies should be able to help by providing the names of adoptive parents. Placing an advertisement in a local newspaper is an effective way of attracting interested people who might want to join. We have included in Appendix B a sample set of by-laws to help in getting started.

Although agencies, social workers and the general public may express interest in the organization, it will likely fail without the initial impetus and constant surveillance of parents. Their motive is the welfare of their own children and children who could be like them.

The Adoption Resource Exchange

This is an organization which serves as a clearinghouse to match children waiting for homes with prospective parents. The aim is to have all the agencies in a given area register with the exchange the children it cannot readily place and the parents it cannot readily serve. There is then created a large pool of children and families which can be matched, even though they are not all referred from the same agency. The exchange also actively recruits families for hard-to-place children. They will utilize parents' groups, the media and public meetings for this purpose.

There are exchanges in several states and one which serves all of North America. They have been particularly successful in finding homes for older, handicapped, mixed-racial children and sibling groups.

One obstacle to the efforts of adoption resource exchanges has been the refusal of some agencies to cooperate by registering children under its care or prospective families in its files. They fear losing their own identity. We hope for the sake of the children whose rights have been ignored for so long that all agencies will be persuaded of the common sense of an exchange and cooperate fully when one is established in its area.

Legislation was introduced but not enacted in the 92nd United States Congress to create a National Adoption Resource Exchange within the Department of Health, Education and Welfare. It has been reintroduced in the 93rd Congress. Such a step would represent a tremendous breakthrough in adoption and significantly improve the chances of thousands of children all over the country for a life of love and security.

Publicity in the Mass Media

Publicity cannot be underestimated in finding homes for children. Unless the public knows about the children, they cannot adopt them. Both adoptive parents' groups and adoption resource exchanges have persuaded radio and television stations to tell not only about adoption in general, but about specific children who need families. Newspapers as well have printed articles or run columns telling of various children waiting in the community.

Media coverage reaches people who may never have considered adopting – they see a picture of a child, which changes an abstract idea into the face of a real person. And the children benefit. For example, the Toronto *Daily Star* carries a daily column with a picture of a waiting child. In 1972, 203 of the children featured had been placed, 3,000 letters were received and 900 other children adopted as a result. Included in that group were three sibling groups of seven children each, with the age range from three months to seventeen years. By any standard, that record is wonderful. Similar pictures and articles will lead to the placement of many more children in the future.

International Adoption and the United Nations

There are homeless children throughout the world. They all deserve families. In Vietnam alone, estimates are that half a million children have been orphaned, at least fifteen thousand of them fathered by Americans.

Many people feel that international adoption is one effective means to improve the lives of these children. As we have seen, some countries are refusing to allow their children to leave for that purpose. We fear that, if this trend continues, the children will suffer. This is because the social and economic needs of some of those countries are so great that they will not have the resources to devote to the financial assistance and child welfare programs necessary to keep families together. What is needed is an international strategy for the welfare of homeless children wherever they may live.

International adoption has always been mired in red tape. The legal problems involved in any state in this country are multiplied in magnitude and difficulty in international adoptions.

Up to now, the United Nations has shown no interest in adoption. However, as a result of an international conference of child welfare agencies, parents and professionals in Milan, Italy, in September, 1971, a resolution was filed in the 1973 General Assembly asking United Nations sponsorship of a worldwide conference on adoption. The conference would disseminate information on adoption to those countries which still do not recognize it, attempt to simplify and make more consistent the various national standards and requirements, and encourage international cooperation for the welfare of children. At this writing, no final action has been taken on the resolution.

We hope that the United Nations will take action. We believe that international adoption is not a second-best alternative but can be a potent force in bringing the world closer together. The challenge to all of us — as individuals, as governments and as a world community — is to be sure that the best interests of all children come first.

In the past, many people have tended to emphasize the problems that might be faced by adopted children and adoptive parents. Professional studies have been made attempting to evaluate the outcome of adoptions and isolate the factors making for success. But despite all that, we are convinced that what matters most are the attitudes and expectations of the people involved — parents, children, relatives, and community. If people look upon adopted children thinking that their "bad blood" or previous trauma will result in permanent problems, then they may create a self-fulfilling prophecy because of the influence their attitudes may have on the child.

The neighborhood that keeps watch on an adopted child to see just how he is "different" doesn't contribute to the healthy growth and adjustment of that child. On the other hand, one that sees an adopted child as just a child will be a positive influence on his normal growth.

If all the children needing families are to find them, adoption should be thought of as a natural way to create a family.

You, the person who wants children, have to be flexible enough to consider all the children who need homes.

You, the grandparents who may be looking forward to a grandchild just like your own child, have to ask yourselves whether it might not be more important to love whatever child your child chooses.

You, the relative or friend or neighbor, have to discard the old secrecy and myths about adoption and realize that it is natural and common.

The future of adoption – and of many of the world's children – is in our hands.

APPENDIXES

Appendix A

ADOPTIVE PARENT GROUPS

ALABAMA

Adoptive Parents Association of Alabama
P.O. Box 5166
Huntsville, Ala. 35805

ARIZONA

Arizona Families for Children
c/o Mrs. Richard L. Keefe
P.O. Box 17951
Tucson, Ariz. 85710

CALIFORNIA

Adopted Parents Association
c/o Roy Hartman, President
813 University Avenue
Burbank, Calif. 91504

Chow, Inc.
c/o Robert McGown, President
3712 Chamberlain Way
Carmichael, Calif. 95608

ADOPTIVE PARENT GROUPS (continued)

CALIFORNIA (continued)

WINGS
c/o Mrs. Mabel Fouse, President
1528 South Mayo Street
Compton, Calif. 90221

Orange County Adoptive Parents' Association
P.O. Box 1314
Huntington Beach, Calif. 92647

Parents' Adoption League
120 East Ocean Boulevard
Long Beach, Calif. 90802

Open Door Society of Los Angeles
c/o Ruth Campbell
3848 Mt. Vernon Drive
Los Angeles, Calif. 90008

Open Door Society of Los Angeles
c/o Mr. and Mrs. Truman Clark
1054 W. 78th Street
Los Angeles, Calif. 90044

Adoptive Parents Association
P.O. Box 66373
Los Angeles, Calif. 90006

Humboldt County Council on Adoptable Children
1371 Whitmire Street
McKinleyville, Calif. 95521

Adoptive Family Association
P.O. Box 1236
Ontario, Calif. 91762

Adoptaides
Panorama Towers, 6th Floor
8155 Van Nuys Boulevard
Panorama City, Calif. 91402

Open Door Society of San Bernardino and Riverside Counties
c/o Mrs. Linda Dunne
250 East Blaine
Riverside, Calif. 92507

Friends of Foster Children
c/o 1 Appaloosa
Rolling Hills, Calif. 90274

The Carriage Trade
1680 Mission Street
San Francisco, Calif. 94103

Families Adopting Interracially (FAIR)
c/o Mrs. Jim Thornton
5147 Forest View Drive
San Jose, Calif. 95129

Adoptive Parent Organization
1062 Grape Street
Sunnyvale, Calif. 94087

Vista Del Mar Adoption Guild
c/o Sue Stutz
5469 Katherine Avenue
Van Nuys, Calif. 91401

Adopted Children's Association of Whittier, Inc.
P.O. Box 797
Whittier, Calif. 94508

ADOPTIVE PARENT GROUPS (continued)

COLORADO

North Area Mother's Club
c/o Mrs. Judy Martine,
President
6238 Ingalls Street
Arvada, Colo. 80002

Parents for All Children
c/o Mr. and Mrs. Bob Sample,
Co-Chairmen
875 Alpine, Apt. #5
Boulder, Colo. 80302

Colorado Adoptive Parents
Association
c/o Mrs. Sam Dalton
1331 West Evans
Denver, Colo. 80223

Lucky Mothers' Club
c/o Mrs. Betty Mayski
3840 S. Narcissus Way
Denver, Colo. 80237

Parents for All Children
c/o Mr. Skip Foseter
355 Balsam
Denver, Colo. 80226

Foothills Mothers' Club
c/o Mrs. Sandra True, President
120 Flower
Lakewood, Colo. 80026

South Suburban Mothers' Club
c/o Mrs. Art Metting, President
4541 South Utica
Littleton, Colo. 80120

CONNECTICUT

Open Door Society of Connecticut, Inc.
P.O. Box 2162
Meriden, Conn. 06450

DELAWARE

Friday's Child
c/o Mrs. Nancy M. Anderson
12 Cornwallis Square
Newark, Del. 19711

DISTRICT OF COLUMBIA

D.C. Metropolitan Area COAC
c/o Mrs. Judy Pope
622 C Street S.E.
Washington, D.C. 20003

ADOPTIVE PARENT GROUPS (continued)

FLORIDA

WE KARE
c/o Mr. and Mrs. William Clark
200 Grace Boulevard
Altamont Springs, Fla. 32701

Susannah K. Becker
(Informal Group)
1209 Obispo
Coral Gables, Fla. 33824

Council on Adoptable Children
P.O. Box 721
Miami, Fla. 33145

GEORGIA

CSRA Adoptive Parents Organization
c/o Mrs. Mogan Wheeler
1652 Pendleton Road
Augusta, Ga. 30904

CSRA Parents Organization
c/o Francis S. Welp, SSG, U.S. Army
1952-A Story Drive
Fort Gordon, Ga. 30905

ILLINOIS

Chosen Parents of Illinois
c/o Mr. and Mrs. Herman H. Harden
P.O. Box 7
Raritan, Ill. 61471

Open Door Society of Illinois, Inc.

514 Hackberry Drive
Arlington Heights, Ill. 60004

McHenry County Chapter
c/o Mr. Rol Jeske
639 Elsinoor Lane
Crystal Lake, Ill. 60014

c/o Mrs. Christine Roos
4850 Lake Park Avenue
Chicago, Ill. 60615

c/o Mr. Jack Kerrill, President
720 Madison Street
Evanston, Ill. 60202

c/o Mr. and Mrs. Jeff Strack
R.R. 2
Sycamore, Ill. 60178

ADOPTIVE PARENT GROUPS (continued)

ILLINOIS (continued)

Council on Adoptable Children of Illinois

c/o Mr. and Mrs. Samuel Mungo
1501 E. Washington
Bloomington, Ill. 61701

1002 S. Busey
Urbana, Ill. 61801

Quad City Council
810 54th Street
Moline, Ill. 61265

INDIANA

Open Door Society
c/o Mr. and Mrs. Daniel Boylan
3934 Fairfield Avenue
Fort Wayne, Ind. 46807

Council on Adoptable Children
c/o Mrs. Moses W. Gray
1929 Copenhaven Drive
Indianapolis, Ind. 46208

The Open Door
P.O. Box 2092
South Bend, Ind. 46615

IOWA

HOLTAP of Iowa
c/o Mr. Warren Cateron
3220 East Douglas
Des Moines, Iowa 50317

Council on Adoptable Children
411 West Clonton
Indianola, Iowa 50125

Iowa City-Cedar Rapids Branch
Open Door Society
c/o Mr. Jerry Musser
R.R. 4
Iowa City, Iowa 52240

Sharing Thru Adoption
c/o Mr. David Alfredson
5418 6th Avenue
Sioux City, Iowa 51106

KANSAS

NCAPO
c/o Rev. Gilbert P. Herrman
Catholic Social Service
2546 20th Street
Great Bend, Kans. 67530

Kansas American Koreans, Inc.
c/o Mr. Larry Sanders
2602 North Monroe
Hutchinson, Kans. 67501

ADOPTIVE PARENT GROUPS (continued)

KANSAS (continued)

Families of Adopted
Mixed-Race Children
c/o Mrs. John Boulton,
President
1721 Kentucky
Lawrence, Kans. 66044

Adoptive Mothers' Club
c/o Mrs. Nancee Price,
Secretary
1206 High
Topeka, Kans. 66604

MAINE

Families for Adoptable Children
Box 416
North Windham, Me. 04062

MARYLAND

Open Door Society of Maryland
P.O. Box 856
Columbia, Md. 21044

Think Adoption (TAD)
5891 Morningbird Lane
Columbia, Md. 21045

NCAPO
c/o Mr. Morton Friedman
9140 Good Luck Road
Lanham, Md. 20801

Council on Adoptable Children
c/o Farley
10513 Bucknell Place
Wheaton, Md. 20902

MASSACHUSETTS

The Open Door Society
of Massachusetts
c/o MARE
600 Washington Street
Boston, Mass. 02111

Adoption Association
of Massachusetts
27 School Street
Boston, Mass. 02108

ADOPTIVE PARENT GROUPS (continued)

MICHIGAN

Grand Rapids Mothers
of Korean Orphans
c/o Mrs. Claude Van Ooyen
3710 Cheyenne Drive
Grandville, Mich. 49418

Muskegon Mothers' Group
c/o Mr. and Mrs. Henry DeJong
1863 Amity Street
Muskegon, Mich. 49442

Beachcombers
c/o Mrs. Raymond Brower
526 James Street
Spring Lake, Mich. 49456

Council on Adoptable Children in Michigan

c/o Mrs. Peter Forsythe
1205 Olivia
Ann Arbor, Mich. 48104

c/o Mrs. Joyce Maisel
19478 Prest
Detroit, Mich. 49235

c/o Mrs. Ronald P. Titsworth
2737 Golfside Lane
Flint, Mich. 48504

1012 Oak Street
Kalamazoo, Mich. 49008

c/o Ms. Barbara Parsons,
Chairman
2125 Clearview Road
Lansing, Mich. 48917

20036 15 Mile Road
Mt. Clemens, Mich. 48043

c/o Mr. and Mrs. James Hawley
830 Airport Road
Muskegon, Mich. 49441

c/o Mrs. John Hoffman
1028 Hoffman Street
Petoskey, Mich. 49770

MINNESOTA

OURS
Organization for a United
Response
3148 Humbold Avenue South
Minneapolis, Minn. 55408

Open Door Society
of Minnesota
3801 Independence Avenue
Minneapolis, Minn. 55427

Associated Parents
c/o Children's Home Society
2230 Como Avenue
St. Paul, Minn. 55108

ADOPTIVE PARENT GROUPS (continued)

MISSOURI

The Adoptive Mothers' Club
c/o Mrs. Raymond Eifert
P.O. Box 382
Illmo, Mo. 63754

Missouri Open Door Society

Headquarters
126 East Washington
Kirkwood, Mo. 63122

Southwest Missouri Chapter
P.O. Box 1856
Bois'D'Arc, Mo. 65612

Central Missouri Chapter
814 Bluff Street
Fulton, Mo. 65251

Kansas City Chapter
P.O. Box 7087
Kansas City, Mo. 64113

Northeast Missouri Chapter
222 East Lafayette
Palmyra, Mo. 63461

Southeast Missouri Chapter
P.O. Box 861
Sikeston, Mo. 63801

St. Louis Chapter
5221 Westminister Place
St. Louis, Mo. 63108

West Central Missouri Chapter
304 Jones Avenue
Warrensburg, Mo. 64093

NEBRASKA

Nebraska Adoptive Parent Club
c/o Mrs. Ann Coyne
1130 West 79th Street
Lincoln, Neb. 68505

NEW HAMPSHIRE

Frontier in Adoption
c/o Mrs. David Carter
R.F.D. 4
Concord, N.H. 03301

Planned Parenthood Association
of Uppervalley
14 Parkhurst Street
Lebanon, N.H. 03766

ADOPTIVE PARENT GROUPS (continued)

NEW JERSEY

Southern New Jersey
Adoptive Parents Organization
c/o Mrs. Rosemary Wells
614 South Drive
Atlantic City, N.J. 08401

Adoptive Mother's Club
of Morris County
c/o Mrs. Carole Walters
114 Flanders Netcong Road
Flanders, N.J. 07836

Adoptive Parents League
of New Jersey, Inc.
15 Inglewood Lane
Matawan, N.J. 07747

Mrs. Allan W. Vliet
18 Altamont Court
Morristown, N.J. 07960

South Jersey Adoption
Association
P.O. Box 583
Pleasantville, N.J. 08232

Frontiers in Adoption
163 Nassau Street
Princeton, N.J. 08540

National Council of Adoptive
Parents Organization
P.O. Box 543
Teaneck, N.J. 07666

Council on Adoptable Children
617 Boulevard
Westfield, N.J. 07090

HOLTAP of New Jersey
P.O. Box 234, Old Highway
Whitehouse, N.J. 08888

Concerned Parents for
Adoption
c/o Mrs. Julie Brohan,
President
200 Parsippany Road
Whippany, N.J. 07981

NEW YORK

Adoptive Parents Committee
Box 93
East Northport, N.Y. 11731

Adoptive Families of
Westchester
P.O. Box 127
Dobbs Ferry, N.Y. 10522

Open Door Society of Greater
New York
c/o Mrs. Faye Caperna
12 Library Lane
Holbrook, N.Y. 11741

Adoptive Parents Committee of
Utica
c/o Mr. Michael Palmiero
New Hartford, N.Y. 13413

Adoptive Parents Committee,
Inc.
210 Fifth Avenue
New York, N.Y. 10010

New York COAC
c/o Mrs. Eve Smith
61 Gramercy Park North
New York, N.Y. 10003

ADOPTIVE PARENT GROUPS (continued)

NEW YORK (continued)

Council of Adoptive Parents
67 Wood Haven Drive
Rochester, N.Y. 14625

Open Door Society of Long Island
c/o Ms. Shirley Damboise
22 Yerk Avenue
Ronkonkoma, N.Y. 11779

Families for the Future
2 Ellsworth Avenue
Scotia, N.Y. 12302

Families for Inter-Racial Adoption
100 DeWitt Road
Syracuse, N.Y. 13214

Parents for All Children of Chautauqua County
25 Chestnut Street
Westfield, N.Y. 14787

Parents for All Children of Western New York
95 Pfohl Place
Williamsville, N.Y. 14221

NORTH CAROLINA

Council on Adoptable Children
c/o Mr. R. Gwyn
Chapel Hill, N.C. 27514

OHIO

Open Door of Cincinnati
3809 Ault Park Avenue
Cincinnati, O. 45208

COAC
c/o Mr. Ed Degenhardt
26580 Mallard Avenue
Euclid, O. 44132

The Adoptive Parents Club
c/o Mrs. Patricia Maulorico, President
1020 Dawnwood Drive
Parma, O. 44134

Council on Adoptable Children
146 Hannum Avenue
Rossford, O. 43460

ACT of Ohio
Adopt A Child Today
Headquarters
P.O. Box 20010
Cleveland, O. 44120

ADOPTIVE PARENT GROUPS (continued)

OHIO (continued)

Chapters

c/o Richard Chartoff
1020 Brayton Avenue
Cincinnati, O. 45215

c/o Dennis M. Gaughn
P.O. Box 20010
Cleveland, O. 44120

c/o Tim Nyros
200 East Oakland Avenue
Columbus, O. 43201

c/o George Edgington
561 North Fairfield Road
Dayton, O. 45430

c/o Michael Freedman
4680 Edson Road
Kent, O. 44240

OREGON

Open Door for Adoptable Children
c/o Mrs. Kathy Nordahl
4875 Garnet Street
Eugene, Ore. 97405

MOKY
c/o Mrs. K. Cutler, President
147 Roundup Drive
Eugene, Ore. 97401

PLAN
842 Southwest Government Street
Newport, Ore. 97365

Open Home Association
c/o Mrs. Lloyd Meskimen
4054 North Colonial
Portland, Ore. 97227

Portland Open Door Society
c/o Mr. Bob Riddle
1736 South East 143rd Street
Portland, Ore. 97233

PENNSYLVANIA

P.O.A.
c/o Mr. Kenneth Westgate
1426 Walnut Street
Allentown, Penna. 18102

Council on Adoptable Children
P.O. Box 3461
Erie, Penna. 16512

ADOPTIVE PARENT GROUPS (continued)

PENNSYLVANIA (continued)

Council on Adoptable Children
P.O. Box 14
Gwynedd, Penna. 19436

Adoptive Parents Group (APG)
c/o Dr. Dennis Lebofsky
14021 Faraday Street
Philadelphia, Penna. 19116

Welcome House Adoptive Parents Group
c/o Ms. Alberta Cohen
R.D. 4, Box 152A
Quakertown, Penna. 18951

Parents of Adopted Children
122 West Springettsburg Avenue
York, Penna. 17403

RHODE ISLAND

Rhode Island Families for Interracial Adoption
433 Elmwood Avenue
Providence, R.I. 02907

SOUTH DAKOTA

COAC
c/o Mr. and Mrs. Ken Knutson
Box 168
Colman, S.D. 57017

TENNESSEE

COAC of Tennessee
c/o Mr. M. Mihal
224 Woodmont
Nashville, Tenn. 37205

TEXAS

COAC of Texas
P.O. Box 33303
Houston, Tex. 77033

Adopted Families of Texas
704 Beta Circle
Pasadena, Tex. 77503

ADOPTIVE PARENT GROUPS (continued)

VERMONT

Room for One More
c/o Mrs. Nancy VanGulden
Williston, Vt. 05495

VIRGINIA

Friend of the Children's Home
Society of Virginia
c/o Mrs. J. R. Williams,
President
311 Clovelly Road
Richmond, Va. 23221

WASHINGTON

Adoptive Family Association
30463 4th Avenue South
Federal Way, Wash. 98002

Open Door Society
312 North Sherman
Olympia, Wash. 98501

Concerned Parents for Children
725 West 6th
Port Angeles, Wash. 98362

Focus on Adoption Committee
c/o Mrs. Marcia W. Baldwin,
Chairman
3337 Hunter Boulevard South
Seattle, Wash. 98144

Interracial Family Association
c/o Mrs. Patricia Ford
3332 Hunter Boulevard South
Seattle, Wash. 98144

Washington Association of
Christian Adoptive Parents
(WACAP)
4424 Francis North
Seattle, Wash. 98103

ADOPTIVE PARENT GROUPS (continued)

WISCONSIN

Open Door Society
1128 Mitscher Avenue
Eau Clair, Wis. 54701

Open Door Society
c/o Mrs. Ralph Carus
3623 South 23rd Street
Milwaukee, Wis. 53221

East-West Circle
c/o Mr. Marvin Winter,
President
712 Marshall Avenue
Milwaukee, Wis. 53172

Open Door Society
c/o Mrs. Reno Kuehnel
Route 1, Box 283
Newton, Wis. 53063

Adoptive Insights
306 North West Avenue
Waukesha, Wis. 53186

CANADA

The Open Door Society, Inc.
1370 Bank Street
Ottawa, Ontario, Canada

La Spadete
1060 Champigny
Duvernay, Laval
Quebec, Canada

National Headquarters
Open Door Society, Inc.
5 Weredale Park
Montreal 215, Quebec, Canada

Families for Children
10 Bowling Green
Pointe Claire 720, Quebec
Canada

Adopt Indian Métis
2340 Albert Street
Regina, Saskatchewan, Canada

EUROPE

Parent to Parent Information on
Adoption Services (PPIAS)
26, Belsize Grove
London NW 3, England

International Committee of
Adoptive Parents
c/o Dr. Giuseppe Cicorella,
President
Viale Brenta, 7
20139 Milan, Italy

ADOPTIVE PARENT GROUPS (continued)

SOUTH AUSTRALIA

Integration League of South Australia (ILSA)
48 Green Street
St. Morris, South Australia

Appendix B

MODEL BY-LAWS OF AN ADOPTIVE PARENTS' ORGANIZATION

ARTICLE I – GENERAL PROVISIONS

1. *Name.* The name of this corporation is Adoptive Parents' Organization, Inc.
2. *Authority.* This corporation is a charitable corporation organized under Chapter ____ of the laws of the State of ______.
3. *Location.* The address and principal office and place of business of the corporation shall be in the City of ______, County of ______, State of ______, or at any other place designated by the Board of Directors and validly filed with the Secretary of State.
4. *Fiscal Year.* The fiscal year of the corporation shall be from the first day of January to the thirty-first day of December, inclusive, each year.
5. *Purposes.* The purposes of this corporation are as follows:
    a. To facilitate the placement of children in need of adoption or foster care;
    b. To disseminate information about adoption and foster care to the general public;
    c. To provide support for adoptive parents, prospective adoptive parents, foster parents, and prospective foster parents;
    d. To work with agencies concerned with adoption and foster care; and

e. To study adoption and foster care laws and procedures and to support necessary changes which are consistent with the goals of this corporation.

6. *Rules of Order.* Unless otherwise prescribed by the Board of Directors, meetings of members and directors shall be conducted in accordance with the latest edition of *Robert's Rules of Order.*

Article II – Membership

1. *Eligibility.* Any person who subscribes to the purposes set forth in Article I and pays his annual dues shall be a member of the corporation. The annual dues shall be fixed by the Board of Directors from time to time.

2. *Rights and Duties of Members.* Each member of the corporation shall have the right to vote at each annual and special meeting of the corporation, and to elect from the membership of the corporation a Board of Directors. Nominations for the election of Directors may be made from the floor only if a notice signed by not less than seven members, giving the name(s) of the nominee(s), is first filed with the Secretary not later than ten days prior to the date of the annual meeting.

Article III – Meetings

1. *Annual and Special Meetings.* The annual meeting of the members of the corporation shall be held at such date and at such place as the Directors shall designate. Written notice of the annual meeting shall be sent by the Secretary to each member, at his usual place of business or residence as shown in the books of the corporation, at least twenty days prior to the meeting.

Special meetings of the corporation may be held at the discretion of the Board of Directors and shall be called within thirty days after receipt by the Directors of a written petition signed by 25 members or 25 percent of the membership, whichever is fewer. Notice of special meetings shall be given by the Secretary in the same manner as required for notices of annual meetings or in any other manner reasonably calculated to notify the members at least three days prior to the date of the special meetings.

2. *Quorum.* Ten members or 10 percent of the membership, whichever is fewer, shall constitute a quorum for the transaction of business at any meeting of the corporation.

3. *Voting.* When a quorum is present at any meeting of the corporation, a majority of the members present and voting shall decide any question unless otherwise provided in these by-laws or otherwise required by law.

Article IV – Committees

1. *Nominating Committee.* At least thirty days prior to every annual meeting of the corporation, the Board of Directors shall appoint a nominating committee consisting of a chairman and two additional members, all of whom shall be members of the corporation and may be Directors, provided, however, that no retiring director shall be appointed to the nominating committee. It shall be the duty of the nominating committee to select and nominate a candidate or candidates for each vacancy created by the expiration of the full term of office of a Director, and for each new Directorship created pursuant to these by-laws, and to present a slate of such candidates for nomination and vote at each annual meeting.

2. *Other Committees.* The Board of Directors may create and terminate any other committees it deems necessary to carry out the purposes of the corporation and shall prescribe their functions. The President of the corporation shall appoint and may remove the Chairman of each committee created by the Directors and may assign to it functions not inconsistent with those specified by the Board. The Chairman of each committee shall appoint and may remove the members of each such committee and shall be responsible for its functioning.

Article V – Directors

1. *Number and Term.* There shall be a Board of Directors of not less than 9 nor more than 36. The number of Directors for any year shall be set by the Board upon appointment of the nominating committee for the election of that year. Directors shall be elected at the annual meeting of the corporation to hold office for terms of three years and until their successors shall be duly elected and qualified. The Directors shall be divided into three classes as nearly equal as possible. At the first annual meeting, Directors shall be elected in such a way that one class shall hold office for one year, a second for two years, and the third for three years, or, in each case, until successors are duly elected and qualified. Thereafter,

only one class to hold office for three years and until successors are duly elected and qualified shall be elected at each succeeding annual meeting. Directors may be elected from candidates nominated as provided herein and may be retiring Directors. In the event the Board is increased as provided herein, candidates for the Directorships thus created shall be elected in as near even distribution to each of the three classes as is possible, as shall be specified by the Board, and their terms shall expire with the terms of those Directors of the class to which they were elected. A candidate may be offered for election to a Directorship in only one class at any one annual meeting.

2. *Powers and Duties.* The Directors shall have and may exercise all of the powers of the corporation except such as are conferred upon the officers and members of the corporation by law and any provision of these by-laws. It shall be the duty of the Board of Directors to manage and control the business and affairs of the corporation and the Board may exercise any powers from time to time granted to the corporation by amendment of existing law. The Board shall be responsible for the performance of any obligation imposed upon the corporation by existing law and any amendments thereto. They may make such further rules for their government as they deem proper, not inconsistent with these by-laws. Immediately following the adjournment of each annual meeting, with the exception of the first meeting of the corporation, the Board serving for the ensuing year shall elect, from its members, a President, Vice-President, Secretary, Treasurer and any other officers it deems necessary to carry out the purposes of the corporation.

3. *Vacancies.* Any vacancy occurring in the Board of Directors may be filled by a vote of a majority of the remaining Directors, though less than a quorum of the whole Board. Directors so elected to fill a vacancy shall serve the unexpired portion of the term vacated and thereafter until their successors are elected and qualified.

4. *Meetings.* A meeting of the Directors shall be held at the annual meeting of the members of the corporation or following the final adjournment thereof. Regular meetings of the Directors may be held at such time and place as the Directors may designate. Special meetings of the Directors may be called by the President or the Secretary, and shall be called upon the petition of any three Directors addressed to the Secretary.

Notice of Directors' meetings shall be sent or given by the Secretary to each Director not less than five days before the time of the meeting. No notice shall be required if the first Directors' meeting is part of the first annual meeting of the corporation or follows the final adjournment thereof. Attendance by a Director at a meeting shall constitute a waiver of notice except where a Director attends a special meeting for the express purpose of objection to the transaction of any business because such special meeting is not lawfully convened. Neither the business to be transacted at nor the purposes of any special meeting of the Board need be specified in the notice or waiver of notice of such meeting.

Except as otherwise provided herein, at any meeting of the Board of Directors, a majority of the whole Board shall constitute a quorum for the transaction of business. Less than a quorum shall have power to adjourn from time to time, until a quorum shall be present. Unless otherwise provided herein, action shall be taken by a majority of the votes cast.

Article VI – Officers

1. *Election, Term and Removal.* Immediately following the final adjournment of each annual meeting of the corporation, with the exception of the first meeting of the corporation, the Board of Directors shall elect from its members a President, Vice-President, Secretary, Treasurer and any other officers deemed necessary by the Board. At the first meeting of the corporation election of the aforementioned officers shall be by the incorporators. Each officer shall serve from the time of his election until the ensuing annual meeting and thereafter until his successor is elected and qualified. Any officer may be removed at any time, with or without cause, by the affirmative vote of two-thirds of the whole Board of Directors.

2. *Vacancies.* Vacancies in any office shall be filled by the Board of Directors for the remainder of the unexpired term so vacated and thereafter until a successor is elected and qualified.

3. *Duties.*

a. *President.* The President shall conduct the management of the corporation subject to the control of the Board of Directors. The President shall preside at all meetings of the members and of the Directors. The President shall have such other powers and perform such other duties as from time to time may be assigned to him by the Board.

b. *Vice-President.* The Vice-President shall have such powers and perform such duties as the Board of Directors may from time to time delegate to him. In the case of the absence or inability to act of the President, the Vice-President shall temporarily act in the place of the President.

c. *Secretary.* The Secretary shall keep an accurate record of the proceedings of all meetings of the corporation and the Board of Directors and record the names of the Directors present at each meeting of the Board. He shall give notice of all meetings of the corporation and all meetings of the Directors as herein provided. He shall be custodian of the records and of the seal of the corporation. He shall have such other powers and perform such other duties as may from time to time be assigned to him by the President and the Board of Directors. In the absence of the Secretary, the Board from time to time may appoint a Secretary pro tempore, to serve until the Secretary resumes his duties.

d. *Treasurer.* The Treasurer shall have responsibility for the custody and safekeeping of all funds and of the financial records of the corporation and shall have charge of their collection, receipt and, in the manner approved by the Board, disbursement. He shall have responsibility for the custody and safekeeping of all securities, shall receive and have authority to sign receipts for all moneys paid to the corporation and shall deposit the same in the name and to the credit of the corporation in such banks or depositaries as the Board of Directors may approve. He shall endorse for collection on behalf of the corporation all checks, drafts, notes and other obligations payable to the corporation, shall disburse the funds of the corporation in the manner prescribed by the Board, shall sign and countersign all notes, endorsements, guaranties and acceptances made on behalf of the corporation when and as directed by the Board, shall keep full and accurate accounts of the transactions of his office in books belonging to the corporation and render to the Board of Directors and the President, whenever they may require, an account of his transactions as Treasurer, and, in general, shall have such other powers and perform such other duties as from time to time may be prescribed by the Board or by the President. The Treasurer may be required to furnish a bond for the faithful performance of his duties. Any expense for a surety on his bond shall be borne by the corporation.

Article VII – Indemnification of Directors, Officers and Employees

1. The corporation shall indemnify any Director, officer or employee, or former Director, officer or employee against any expense

or liability occasioned by reason of being or having been such Director, officer, or employee, if, in the judgment of a majority of the whole Board of Directors, such indemnity ought equitably to be made. Such indemnification shall be made only to the extent authorized by law.

Article VIII – Amendments

1. These by-laws may be amended at any annual or special meeting of the corporation by a vote of two-thirds of those present and voting, provided that notice of the substance of such amendment has been given in the call of the meeting.

Appendix C

MODEL REFORM LAWS

1. Uniform Surrender Document and Procedure Making the Surrender Irrevocable Once Executed

A decree of adoption shall not be made, except as provided in this chapter, without the written consent of the child to be adopted, if above the age of twelve; of the child's spouse, if any; of the lawful parents, who may be previous adoptive parents, or surviving parent; or of the mother only if the child was born out of wedlock and not previously adopted. A person whose consent is hereby required shall not be prevented from being the adoptive parent.

Such written consent shall be executed no sooner than the fourth calendar day after the date of birth of the child to be adopted. It shall be attested and subscribed before a notary public in the presence of two competent witnesses, one of whom shall be selected by said person. The agency or person receiving custody shall act as guardian of the child until such time as a court of competent jurisdiction appoints a guardian or grants a petition for adoption. Execution of such consent shall be carried out in a manner which shall preserve privacy and confidentiality. A copy of said consent shall be filed with the department of public welfare. A consent executed in accordance with the provisions of this section shall be final and irrevocable from date of execution.

The form of such consent shall be as follows:

I, as the (relationship) of (name of child), age , of the sex, born in (place of birth), on (date of birth), do hereby voluntarily and unconditionally surrender (child) to the care and custody of (agency or person receiving custody) for the purpose of adoption or such other disposition as may be made by a court of competent jurisdiction. I waive notice of any legal proceeding affecting the custody, guardianship, adoption or other disposition of (child). I UNDERSTAND THAT THIS SURRENDER IS FINAL AND CANNOT BE REVOKED.

/s/ (person giving consent)

On this day of 19 , before me personally came and appeared and in my presence duly executed the foregoing instrument, and (he, she) acknowledged to me that (he, she) executed the same as (his, her) free act and deed, fully cognizant of its irrevocability.

Date

State of

Notary Public

County of

Signed by (name of person giving consent) as (his, her) freely executed consent in the presence of each of us, and of each other, who thereafter have hereunto signed our names as witnesses. /s/

Address

/s/

Address

2. Procedure for Terminating the Right of Parents to Consent to Adoption

(a) Whenever a petition for adoption is filed by a person having the care or custody of a child, the consent of the persons named in section two, other than that of the child, shall not be required if:

(*i*) the person to be adopted is eighteen years of age or older, or if

(*ii*) the court hearing the petition finds that the allowance of the petition is in the best interests of the child, as defined in paragraph (c).

(b) The department of public welfare or any licensed child care agency may commence a proceeding, independent of a petition for adoption, in the probate court of ______ county or any other county in which said department or agency maintains an office, to dispense with the need for consent of any person named in section two to the adoption of a child in the care or custody of said department or agency. Notice of such proceeding shall be given to such person in a manner prescribed by the court. The court shall issue a decree dispensing with the need for said consent or notice of any petition for adoption of such child subsequently sponsored by said department or agency if it finds that the best interests of the child as defined in paragraph (c) will be served by said decree. Pending a hearing on the merits of a petition filed under this paragraph, temporary custody may be awarded to the petitioner.

(c) In determining whether the best interests of the child will be served by granting a petition for adoption without requiring certain consent as permitted under paragraph (a), the court shall consider the ability, capacity, fitness and readiness of the child's parents to assume parental responsibility and shall also consider the ability, capacity, fitness and readiness of the petitioners under paragraph (a) to assume such responsibilities.

In determining whether the best interests of the child will be served by issuing a decree dispensing with the need of consent as permitted under paragraph (b), the court shall consider the ability, capacity, fitness and readiness of the child's parents to assume parental responsibility, and shall also consider the plan proposed by the department or other agency initiating the petition.

If said child has been in the care of the department or a licensed child care agency for more than one year, in each case irrespective of incidental communications or visits from his parents, irrespective of a court decree awarding custody of said child to another and notwithstanding the absence of a court decree ordering said parents or other person to pay for the support of said child, there shall be a presumption that the best interests of the child will be served by granting a petition for adoption as permitted under paragraph (a) or by issuing a decree dispensing with the need for consent as permitted under paragraph (b).

3. Rights of the Unwed Father

Whenever the mother of a child born out of wedlock has surrendered the child, notice of such surrender shall be given to the father of the child if, before or within seven days of such surrender, he has filed a paternal responsibility claim with the department of public welfare which shall acknowledge paternity of a particular child and accept all obligations of paternity.

Any individual or agency receiving a child for the purpose of adoption shall search the paternal responsibility claims on file with the department, and if a claim has been filed with respect to such child in accordance with the requirements of the preceding paragraph, then the individual or agency receiving the child shall notify the father of its receipt and the county of its location, by registered mail to the address stated on the father's claim. A copy of the consent executed by the mother shall be appended to said notice.

If paternity has not previously been determined, a proceeding to determine paternity shall be given speedy consideration by the probate court. If the person is found, or has been previously found, to be the father of the child, and has a suitable plan for its custody, then the court may award the father custody. If the person is found not to be the father of the child, or has no suitable plan for its custody, he shall have no further rights with respect to such child. Any costs incurred for the temporary care of the child pending the outcome of the proceedings shall be borne by the putative father.

4. Financial Subsidies to Adoptive Parents

The department of ———— shall establish a program for financial subsidy to certain adopting parents to facilitate the adoption of children who are in foster care with the department or with any licensed foster care agency, and who would not otherwise receive appropriate adoptive placement. Said department shall adopt rules and regulations to implement the provisions of this act. Financial subsidy may consist of payments either for the general support of such children, or for their medical or remedial care, or both.

Eligibility for payments for such support or care of children to be adopted shall be determined in accordance with income and resource limitations based upon the number of persons, including the child or children to be adopted, in the household, and upon the out-of-pocket expenses for the medical and remedial care of said child or children. Only adoptive parents who have made arrangements with the department prior to adoption shall be eligible to receive post-adoption assistance under this act.

Payments made under this act shall not exceed those currently authorized by the department for a comparable child or children in family foster care.

5. Tips for Legislative Reform

1. Gather people who are able to
   (a) define the problem with existing law in terms of its practical effect;
   (b) evaluate whether legislative change is necessary to solve the problem; and
   (c) understand the attitudes and procedures of the law-making bodies.
2. Identify the likely opposition and the likely supporters.
3. Choose a legislative sponsor who
   (a) understands and is interested in the problem;
   (b) is likely to have influence with the likely opposition; and
   (c) is respected by his colleagues and by the media.
4. Acquire a skilled draftsman able to draft a bill with the likely opposition and alternative strategies in mind.
5. Always have an acceptable compromise ready.
6. Inform fully the potential opposition and try to obtain their support, or, at least, their silent acquiescence.
7. Solicit firm commitments of support from all interested groups and individuals and plan specific manifestation of that support (e.g., written endorsements, contact with legislators).
8. Carefully plan legislative strategy with special emphasis on orchestrating the hearing and timing publicity.
9. Maintain daily contact with the progress of the bill via reports from the sponsor(s) and contact with key legislators where appropriate.
10. Do everything possible without compromising essential goals to eliminate important opposition and to obtain a favorable report after hearing.
11. Be sensitive to the appropriate time for a decision on whether an acceptable compromise is necessary and possible – prolonged indecision can waste time necessary for preparing for a real fight, yet hasty combativeness can lead to unnecessary failure.
12. Never relax constituent contact and pressure until the battle is clearly won or clearly lost.

NOTES TO CHAPTERS

Chapter 4

1. Joseph Reid, "Principles, Values and Assumptions Underlying Adoptive Practices," *Social Work,* 2 (June 1957): 22, 24; Erik Erikson, "Growth and Crises of the Healthy Personality," *Psychological Issues,* 1 (1957): 50; John Bowlby, *Maternal Care and Mental Health* (Geneva: World Health Organization, 1951).

Chapter 7

1. National Center for Social Statistics, U.S. Department of Health, Education and Welfare, *Adoptions in 1969, Adoptions in 1970, Adoptions in 1971, Adoptions in 1972* (Washington, D.C., 1970, 1971, 1972, 1973).
2. Ibid.

Chapter 9

1. National Center for Social Statistics, U.S. Department of Health, Education and Welfare, *Adoptions in 1970, Adoptions in 1971* (Washington, D.C., 1971, 1972).
2. Judy Klemesrud, "Adoption Costs Soar as Births Decline," New York *Times,* February 20, 1973.
3. Helen L. Witmer, Elizabeth Herzog, Eugene A. Weinstein and Mary E. Sullivan, *Independent Adoptions: A Follow-up Study* (New York: Russell Sage Foundation, 1963), pp. 111–114.
4. United States Senate, Hearings on Interstate Adoption Practices before the Subcommittee to Investigate Juvenile Delinquency of the Committee on the Judiciary, 84th Congress, 1st session, July 15 and 16 and November 14 and 15, 1955 (U.S. Government Printing Office, Washington, D.C., 1956).
5. Ibid., November 14 and 15, pp. 72–73 (statement of Ernest A. Mitler, special counsel to the Subcommittee to Investigate Juvenile Delinquency).
6. Howard Bluth, "Factors in the Decision to Adopt Independently," *Child Welfare,* vol. 46, no. 11 (November 1967), pp. 504–513.

7. Lurana Snow, *Report on Independent Adoption* (Governor's Commission on Adoption and Foster Care, Commonwealth of Massachusetts, September 1, 1972), pp. 22–26.

8. Donald Brieland, *An Experimental Study of the Selection of Adoptive Parents at Intake* (Child Welfare League of America, 1959); Henry Mass, "The Successful Adoptive Parent Applicants," *Social Work* (January 1960), p. 5; *Standards for Adoption Service*, rev. ed. (Child Welfare League of America, 1968), pp. 44–46.

9. Witmer, Herzog, Weinstein and Sullivan, *Independent Adoptions*, p. 358.

10. Ibid., pp. 354, 355.

11. Albert J. Rosenstein, "Comparative Study of Role Conflict, Marital Adjustment, and Personality Configuration of Private and Agency Adoptive Parents" (Ph.D. dissertation, University of Michigan, as appearing in *Dissertation Abstracts*, vol. 20, no. 10 [1960], pp. 4208–4209).

Chapter 10

1. National Center for Social Statistics, U.S. Department of Health, Education and Welfare, *Child Welfare Statistics*, 1968, 1969, 1970 (Washington, D.C., 1969, 1970, 1971).

2. Alfred Kadushin, *Child Welfare Services* (New York: Macmillan, 1967), p. 364.

3. Alan R. Gruber, *Foster Home Care in Massachusetts* (Boston: Governor's Commission on Adoption and Foster Care, Commonwealth of Massachusetts, 1973), pp. 17–18.

4. *Report to Governor Sargent* (Boston: Governor's Commission on Adoption and Foster Care, March 14, 1973).

5. Leon Eisenberg, "The Sins of the Fathers: Urban Decay and Social Pathology," *American Journal of Orthopsychiatry*, vol. 32, no. 1 (1962); Rosemary Dinnage, *Foster Home Care, Faults and Fallacies: A Review of Research in the United States, Western Europe, Israel and Great Britain Between 1948 and 1966* (London: Longmans [in association with the National Bureau for Cooperation in Child Care], 1967).

Chapter 11

1. *1970 Survey of Adoption of Black Children* (Portland, Ore.: Boys and Girls Aid Society of Oregon, 1970).

CHAPTER 14

1. Ethel Branham, "One Parent Adoptions," *Children*, vol. 17, no. 3 (May–June 1970).

CHAPTER 15

1. U.S. Immigration and Naturalization Service, *Annual Report*, Fiscal Years 1970, 1971, 1972 (Washington, D.C., 1970, 1971, 1972).

CHAPTER 16

1. Margaret Mead, *Sex and Temperament* (New York: New American Library, 1935), p. 48.
2. Ibid., pp. 149–150.
3. Albert Kocourek and John H. Wigmore, "Evolution of Law," *Sources of Ancient and Primitive Law* (Boston: Little, Brown, 1915), p. 387.
4. Exodus 2:10; see also Esther 2:5–8, in which Mordecai adopts his niece Esther.
5. Sir Frederick Pollock and Frederic William Maitland, *The History of English Law Before the Time of Edward I*, 2nd ed. (Cambridge: The University Press, 1898), II, 398.
6. Edmund S. Morgan, *The Puritan Family*, 2nd ed. (New York: Harper and Row, 1966), p. 77.
7. Arthur Wallace Calhoun, *A Social History of the American Family* (New York: Barnes and Noble, 1960), I, 306–307.
8. Charles Loring Brace, *The Best Method of Disposing of Pauper and Vagrant Children* (1859), pp. 13–14.
9. *Non-She-Po* v. *Wa-Win-Ta*, 37 Oregon 213, 62 Pac. 15 (1900); *Henry* v. *Taylor*, 16 S.D. 424, 93 N.W. 641 (1903).
10. *Kiaiaina* v. *Kahawu*, 3 Hawaii 368 (1871); *Estate of Nakupa*, 3 Hawaii 420 (1873).
11. William Henry Whitmore, *The Law of Adoption in the United States and Especially in Massachusetts* (Albany: Joel Munsell, 1876), p. 74.
12. Ibid.

CHAPTER 17

1. See Comment, "The Adoption of Baby Lenore: Two Interpretations of a Child's Best Interests," *Journal of Family Law*, 11 (1971): 285, n. 29.

2. Joseph Reid, "Principles, Values and Assumptions Underlying Adoptive Practices," *Social Work*, 2 (June 1957): 22, 24; Erik Erikson, "Growth and Crises of the Healthy Personality," *Psychological Issues*, 1 (1957): 50; John Bowlby, *Maternal Care and Mental Health* (Geneva: World Health Organization, 1951).

3. *People ex rel. Scarpetta* v. *Spence-Chapin Adoption Service*, 36 App. Div. 2d 524, 317 N.Y.S. 2d 928, *aff'd.*, 28 N.Y. 2d 185, 321 N.Y.S. 2d 65 (1971); *Scarpetta* v. *DeMartino*, No. 71 975 (Fla. 3d Dist. Ct. App. Sept. 28, 1971).

4. 321 N.Y.S. 2d at 70.

5. Leon Yarrow, "Separation from Parent During Early Childhood," in *Review of Child Development Research*, ed. Martin L. Hoffman and Lois W. Hoffman (New York: Russell Sage Foundation, 1964); Robert G. Patton, *Growth Failure in Maternal Deprivation* (New York, 1963).

CHAPTER 18

1. *Stanley* v. *Illinois*, 405 U.S. 645 (1972).

2. *Stanley* v. *Illinois*, 405 U.S. at 651.

CHAPTER 19

1. Helen Simpson, "The Unfit Parent: Conditions under which a Child May Be Adopted without the Consent of his Parents," *University of Detroit Law Journal*, 39 (1962): 347.

CHAPTER 20

1. *Petitions of Goldman*, 331 Mass. 647 (1954).

2. *Ellis* v. *McCoy*, 332 Mass. 254 (1955); see the account in New York *Times*, July 9, 1957, p. 33, col. 1.

3. *In re Maxwell*, 4 N.Y. 2d 429 (1958); see also *Cooper* v. *Hinrichs*, 10 Ill. 2d 269 (1957), and *In re Adoption of a Minor*, 355 Mo. 1222 (1947).

4. *Purinton* v. *Jamrock*, 195 Mass. 187, 199–200 (1907).

5. *Pereira* v. *Pereira*, Probate Court, Bristol County, Mass. No. D-16741 (1954).

6. *Matter of Santos*, 105 N.Y.S. 2d 716.

7. *Petitions of Goldman*, 331 Mass. 647 (1954).

8. Anson Phelps Stokes and Leo Pfeffer, *Church and State in the United States* (New York: Harper and Row, 1964), p. 446.

9. Brooklyn *Tablet*, August 1, 1953, p. 1 (as quoted in Pfeffer, "Religion in the Upbringing of Children," *Boston University Law Review*, 35 [1955]: 335, n. 17).

10. Public Testimony of Msgr. Leo Battista, Executive Director, Catholic Charitable Bureau of Worcester, on H. 4715 before Joint Committee on Social Welfare, General Court of Massachusetts, March 1969.

11. Opinion of Justice Qua in *Petitions of Goldman*, 331 Mass. 647 at 649 (1954).

12. John Bowlby, *Maternal Care and Mental Health* (Geneva: World Health Organization, 1951), p. 101.

13. Child Welfare League of America, *Standards for Adoption Service*, rev. ed. (New York, 1968), sec. 2.6.

14. *In re Adoption of E*, 112 N.J. Super. 326, Essex Cty. Ct. 1970.

15. New York *Times*, November 1970.

16. *In re Adoption of E*, 59 N.J. 36 (1971).

17. Massachuestts St. 1969, Ch. 404; Md. Ann. Code, Art. 16, Sec. 67 (b), Supp. 1970; Maine Rev. Stat. Ann., Title 22, Sec. 3795, Supp. 1970.